U0738569

中国文化万花筒

Chinese Cultural Kaleidoscope

张月红　编著

Yuehong (Helen) Zhang

ORCID: http://orcid.org/0000-0001-8702-909X

图书在版编目（CIP）数据

中国文化万花筒 = Chinese Cultural Kaleidoscope：
汉、英 / 张月红编著. — 杭州：浙江大学出版社，2016.5
ISBN 978-7-308-15903-6

Ⅰ．①中… Ⅱ．①张… Ⅲ．①中华文化－汉、英
Ⅳ．①K203

中国版本图书馆CIP数据核字(2016)第111084号

中国文化万花筒

张月红　编著

策划编辑	张　琛
责任编辑	韦　伟　林汉枫
责任校对	仲亚萍
装帧设计	方宇珑
出版发行	浙江大学出版社
	（杭州市天目山路148号　　邮政编码　310007）
	（网址：http://www.zjupress.com）
排　　版	杭州林智广告有限公司
印　　刷	浙江印刷集团有限公司
开　　本	787mm×1092mm　1/32
印　　张	8
字　　数	160千
版 印 次	2016年5月第1版　2016年5月第1次印刷
书　　号	ISBN 978-7-308-15903-6
	DOI：10.1631/ZUP.B978-7-308-15903-6
定　　价	46.00元

For our international scholars and their children,
as well as anyone who enjoys Chinese culture

献给国际同行评审的学者们及他们的孩子，
以及全世界欣赏中国文化的人们

foreword

前　言

China's Cultural History— In Foreigners' Eyes

Whilst modern China and its phenomenal economic growth since 1978 and the "Reform and Opening Up" are known to most of us, because hardly a day goes by without an economic or political news headline about China, we are far less familiar with Chinese history and culture. "Chinese civilization originates in an antiquity so remote that we vainly endeavour to discover its commencement", so said the 19th century French missionary and traveller Abbé Régis-Évariste Huc.

China suffered terribly in the 19th century and first half of the 20th at the hands of foreign invaders and was reduced to a sorrowful state.

However, I always say that for any visitor to modern China, a visit to the Shanghai Museum in People's Square is a must or, similarly, to the National Museum of China in Beijing. The visitor will see how advanced a civilization this was even long before the birth of Christ. Not for nothing is the Chinese name for this country *Zhongguo*,

外国人眼里的中国文化

相较于悠悠漫长的上下五千年的中国文化历史，作为西方人，我们更熟悉现代中国，因为从 1978 年改革开放以来，她以惊人的经济增长而被世人皆知。几乎每一天，中国都会成为世界经济或政治要闻栏目中的主角。记得 19 世纪法国传教士和旅行家古伯察神父来到中国时所说，"若想真正读懂中华文化的博大精深，抑或纵深探究华夏文明的历史起源，对一个西方人来说可以想象达到这一步的距离有多远？"

在世人的记忆中，19 世纪和 20 世纪前半叶的中国受尽了西方列强的蹂躏和掠夺。那时的她，可谓是国力积弱贫穷，民生苦不堪言。

但是，我总对朋友们说，任何一个游客来到现代中国的上海，地处人民广场的上海博物馆是一定要去参观的，就如同到了北京，中国国家博物馆是必须要进去感受的。因为在这里，作为一个外国参观者，您会亲临其境，印象深刻地相信这样一个事实：在基督诞生之前的几千年里，以农耕为主的华夏子民就以一种"中央王国"的心态自居，农耕、繁衍、生息在黄河流域，那是一种何等的文明！

meaning "The Middle Kingdom". China truly was the centre of the world for an exceedingly long time.

Here are some interesting comparisons: Go back in time a mere 650 years to the founding of the Ming Dynasty in 1368. For nearly three centuries few would argue that this civilization was the world's most advanced. Look at the priceless artifacts on display in those museums in Shanghai and Beijing. Admittedly, the Ming Dynasty came to a sad end but compare, for example, Nanjing with London in the early 15th century. The former had a population of more than half a million, London less than fifty thousand, where one in three children died before the age of one. The city walls of Nanjing, which still largely stand today, are the most impressive I have ever seen, not just in their strength but also their length. During the Ming Dynasty scholarship flourished and the Yongle Emperor made Nanjing a centre of learning. The encyclopedia he commissioned finally filled over eleven thousand volumes, which was the earliest encyclopedia (1408) in the world, even earlier than the *Encyclopaedia Britannica* (1768) by more

同时你会被这些事实深深震撼并确信，很久很久以前，中国，这个象征着国家名字的"Zhongguo"，意为"中央王国"，不仅真实地存在着，而且在世界历史的长河中，曾是一个相当长时间的"中心"！

这里还想从一个外国人的视角谈一些有趣的见闻及心理比较。时间回溯到距今近 650 年，于 1368 年建国的大明王朝。当今世界文化圈内，对于明朝当时的文明水平居于世界领先地位的共识，在近三个世纪内的史学家们几乎少有争辩。对此，上海和北京的这两个博物馆所展出的那些价值连城的明朝文物也是铁证。当然，明朝在 1644 年悲凉地迎来了它近三个世纪辉煌的寿终。如若比较 15 世纪南京与伦敦两城的聚居人口，你会惊讶地发现，前者超过五十万，而后者不足五万。更让人唏嘘悲叹的是，当时伦敦城内每三个孩子中就会有一个孩子不到周岁而夭亡。再看建筑实力，我亲眼所见，大明王朝的城墙，依然霸气地屹立在 21 世纪的南京城内，那城墙的长度也令我过目不忘。这些都足以见证明王朝的实力与强大。更让我难忘的还有明朝兴盛的讲学制度，以及永乐皇帝朝下的南京城已成为当时文化交流的中心。还有在他的皇令下，当朝大兴科举与编修古籍，1408 年已将百科全书——《永乐大典》

than 360 years.

The Scottish economic historian Niall Ferguson in his book *Civilization*, the 2011 edition published by Penguin Books, reminds us that, at this time, the English, when not fighting each other, were in wars with the Scots, and in The Hundred Years War with France. Indeed, all Europe was torn by wars and in the east 1453 saw the fall of Constantinople, the end of the Byzantine Empire and the ascendancy of the Ottomans and Islam. But China was flourishing while Europe was suffering.

Of course, this all changed. Global power shifted from East to West but it took a long time. On the orders of King George III of England, Lord Macartney's abortive visit to China only took place in 1793 when he tried to interest the Qianlong Emperor in the new products of European science.

It is hoped that this book will throw some light on China's rich cultural history, including Chinese philosophy, and encourage further reading.

The origin of this book is related to the managing editor of the English language science journal of Zhejiang

编撰装订达 11000 册之多，成为世界有史以来最早出版的百科全书，比英国《大英百科全书》(1768) 要早 360 年。

而此时的欧洲，战马嘶叫，战火连连。从苏格兰经济历史学家尼尔·弗格森 2011 年出版的《文明》一书中可见一斑。譬如，当时的英国几乎没有一天停止过战争，邻与苏格兰连年征战，远与隔海的法国战出了史上赫赫有名的"英法百年大战"。那时的战火把整个欧洲生生地撕裂了！向东看去，人们不会忘记 1453 年君士坦丁堡的陷落，千年不可一世的拜占庭帝国（即东罗马帝国）就那样轰然倒下了。继之是几百年奥斯曼帝国与伊斯兰教的盛行与衰落。总之，林林总总道不尽这段欧洲战争史。相较战火不断的欧洲，地球东方的中国，如上所述的大明王朝，却是另一派蒸蒸日上，文化繁荣，百姓安居的生活景象。这就是历史，也是不可思议的人类史。

地球自转的规律依次是东方不亮西方亮。时过境迁，一切都在变。几个世纪后，西方的科学与工业实力日见兴盛。尽管这个过程不短，但地球上显示国力强大的趋势的确自东转向了西。还记得 18 世纪末，英国国王乔治三世派遣的外交使节马戛尔尼勋爵对中国的访问几近流产。缘由是他试图让乾隆皇帝去接受并相信欧洲科学发明的现

University Press, based in the city of Hangzhou, famous for its West Lake, visited by Marco Polo during the Yuan Dynasty, and whose statue stands on the lakeside today. He described the city as being "beyond dispute the finest and noblest in the world". Hangzhou is again a wealthy place. It has become one of the most affluent cities in modern China.

Every year, at Christmas time in the West, the managing editor of this journal sends a greetings card to her editorial board members who are scattered around the world, including many in Europe and North America. But along with the card there is other material, such as a collection of special Chinese stamps, or maybe something about the writings and importance of Confucius. Always something about Chinese history and culture is included. For Christmas 2015 it was a booklet entitled "The Culture of Chinese Festivals and Holidays", again with special stamps included and explaining events like the Spring Festival, Tomb-Sweeping Day, the Dragon Boat Festival and others. It is a small but important way of reminding people that China has an illustrious past of which it is

实、工业产品的先进，并不断地演示这些新产品的努力失败了。这件事就发生在 1793 年北京的皇城宫。

希望这本书的出版将会引发我们对丰富的中国文化史，包括中国哲学和中国民俗等的浓厚兴趣，激发我们进一步去阅读中国的过去，了解她的现在。

其实，这本书的出版与一位英文学术期刊的总编辑有关，她也是我的中国同事。作为一个西方出版人，退休后，我在中国杭州的浙江大学出版社做了几年的英文编辑。其间，亲眼目睹了中国最美城市——杭州的美丽。正如元代路过杭州的意大利旅行家马可·波罗所说："杭州是世上毫无争议的尊贵与秀美之城。"他的雕像，如同他真人一般至今还恋恋不舍地望着烟雨朦胧的西湖，回味着天堂的魅力。杭州也是一个富庶之地，它已成为现代中国最富裕的城市之一。

这几年里，每当西方最隆重的节日——圣诞节来临的前夕，我能亲身感受到，这个期刊编辑总是在策划编撰不同主题的"中国文化小名片"，与她的同事们忙于给分散在世界各地的审稿专家，包括许多在欧洲和北美的期刊编委会成员邮寄这份表达"中国文化"的圣诞礼物。伴随着这书香的文化小册，还有与主题相配的中国小邮票——这

proud, and which helps explain why it again seeks to be an important player on the world stage.

Ian McIntosh

March 26, 2016

(The preface is by a former editor of learned journals from the UK who has spent long periods in China since 2008 assisting the editorial staff at Zhejiang University Press, in Hangzhou. He has travelled quite widely in China and visited many places of historical and cultural interest.

Ian McIntosh先生从英国一家出版社退休后，2008年来浙江大学出版社做了几年英文编辑。其间他只身一人游历了中国诸多的历史名城和文化圣地，可谓有些体会，为本书写了前言。)

种组合可谓是天衣无缝的"中国文化小名片"点睛。譬如《中国哲学——古代六大思想家》的小册子，不仅让每位接收者从邮票中满足了对孔夫子"模样"的想象力，也略知孔子的《论语》对中华民族文化思想的影响力。简言之，这些"圣诞礼物"恰好契合了中国历史与文化，风俗与民情的表达，满足了我们这些蓝眼睛的好奇心。再如，2015年的"圣诞礼物"就是一份介绍中国节日，也称为"年"的文化小册子。它精致而美丽，从中你不仅知道了中国传统的节日为春节、元宵、清明和端午等，也记住了中国的国庆节是每年的十月一日，有3天假期，真的是一种文化的享受。

这种表达不仅很暖人意，也是一种不经意的细致，向世人慢慢地述说着华夏民族辉煌的历史、灿烂的文化、迷人的民俗……从中或许诠释了当今中国之所以又一次成为世界舞台上的重要角色的缘由吧。

Ian McIntosh 写于 2016 年 3 月 26 日

本书作者译

Acknowledgments

致 谢

Acknowledgments

First and foremost, the author would like not only to thank Ian McIntosh for checking the English throughout the whole book, but also the graphic designer, Yulong Fang who graduated from the China Academy of Art in 1999, and collaborated with the author to complete the design of the series, including all illustrations in this book. Thanks also to my editorial team, HF Lin, YZ Miao, JL Zeng, XX Zhang, SQ Yang, Q Ye, ZY Zhai, F Zhang and XB Song for their data-collecting and proofreading. Finally, the author would like to thank the providers of all the references used in this book, in print or online.

Last but not least, I would like to thank my daughter who called this book a "Chinese Cultural Kaleidoscope", meaning that not only can it makes people see the pageant in the progress of the Chinese nation and its cultural heritage, but also implies that we are grateful and happy for this ever-changing kaleidoscopic beauty.

致　谢

　　作者非常感谢英国的资深出版人 Ian McIntosh 先生对本书的英文撰稿做了细致的润色。更要感谢 1999 年毕业于中国美院的方宇珑女士与作者多年的默契合作，不仅完成了作者所编撰的一系列主题文化册的美术设计，并对本书所有图形的设计与处理倾注了才华。同时，还要感谢作者的编辑同事林汉枫、缪弈洲、张欣欣、曾建林、杨树启、叶青和翟自洋，以及张帆、宋晓博对本书的资料收集、整理、排版和校对等诸多工作的支持和帮助。当然，作者诚恳地致谢本书所有参考资料和图片的提供者，无论其来自网络还是印刷作品等 (见文中的标引及各章的脚注)，作者在此一并对原创作者表示感谢！正是贵方的智慧和成果启发和成全了作者，编撰了这本浅浅的中国文化小册子。

　　最后，作者不忘感谢女儿给本书起名为 "Chinese Cultural Kaleidoscope (中国文化万花筒)"，她寓意上下五千年的华夏文明每一个触角都是一个灿烂的光点，折射出中华民族的壮丽与华夏历史的沧桑。而面对这色彩斑斓、变化万千的中国元素，留在心里的就是感动、感谢和感恩！

Contents

Chapter 1   The Civilization of China

HuaXia, China   / 002

    The background to Chinese characters—The sole

        survivors of the world's oldest four writing systems   / 006

Chinese Culture Cards   / 010

    The Terracotta Warriors of the Qin Dynasty   / 012

    The Great Wall   / 014

    The Temple of Heaven   / 016

    Hemudu Culture Site   / 018

    Painting & Calligraphy—Works by Zheng Banqiao   / 020

    Beijing Opera   / 024

    Ancient musical instruments   / 026

    Chinese pottery   / 028

    Chinese culture's wise man—Confucius   / 030

Chapter 2   The Land of China

Geography of China   / 036

Children's Folk Song—*Chinese Rooster Map*   / 040

Chinese People's Family   / 044

Our Beloved Motherland /046

    Yellow and Yangtze rivers—mother rivers /046

    The five sacred mountains in China /048

    Tibet and its Potala Palace /050

    Hong Kong /054

    Macau /056

    Taiwan /058

    The origins of geographical names of the other provinces,
cities and regions /060

Chapter 3   Selection from Chinese Classical Literary Works

Romance of the Three Kingdoms /086

The Water Margin /088

The Peony Pavilion /090

Chapter 4   Selection from Ancient Chinese Buildings

Wonderful Ancient Chinese Buildings /094

    Pagoda of Six Harmonies /094

    Great Wild Goose Pagoda /096

    Zhenguo Pagoda /098

    Youguo Pagoda /100

    Yellow Crane Tower /102

Yueyang Tower   / 102

Tengwang Pavilion   / 104

Penglai Pavilion   / 104

Beautiful Ancient Chinese Waterside Towns   / 106

Zhouzhuang Town   / 106

Tongli Town   / 106

Wuzhen Town   / 108

Nanxun Town   / 108

Luzhi Town   / 110

Xitang Town   / 110

Chapter 5　China's Folk Culture

The Culture of Chinese Festivals and Holidays   / 114

Spring Festival (or Chinese New Year)   / 116

Lantern Festival   / 120

Tomb-Sweeping Day (or Qingming Festival)   / 122

Dragon Boat Festival (or Duanwu Festival)   / 124

Mid-Autumn Festival   / 126

New Year's Day   / 128

International Labour Day   / 130

International Children's Day   / 132

National Day   / 134

Blessings Culture / 136

Good fortune—Fu / 138

Prosperity or emolument—Lu / 138

Longevity—Shou / 140

Happiness—Xi / 140

Chinese Zodiac / 142

Chapter 6 The Chinese Style of Writing

Four Treasures of Study in China / 152

Chinese Calligraphy / 154

The "Four Gentlemen" in Painting / 158

Chapter 7 Chinese Philosophy

Six Ancient Chinese Thinkers of the

Pre-Qin Period / 166

Sage of Chinese culture

—Confucius (551–479 BC) / 172

The idealistic wing of Confucianism

—Mencius (c 371–289 BC) / 176

The realistic wing of Confucianism

—Xun Zi (c 298–238 BC) / 178

The main founder of Taoism

Lao Zi (c 571 471 BC) / 180

The greatest person of the early Taolists

　　—Zhuang Zi (c 369–286 BC)   / 184

The first opponent of Confucius

　　—Mo Zi (c 479–381 BC)   / 186

Chapter 8　A Sight of Modern China—Beijing 2008 Olympic Games

Beijing 2008 Olympic Games—China's Strengths   / 190

Official Mascot—Fuwas' Story   / 192

Chapter 9　Overlooking the Hometown—Hangzhou

Paradise on Earth—Beautiful Hangzhou   / 202

Longjing Tea Fragrance and Lu Yü's *The Tea Classic*   / 206

Waterside Towns Surrounding Hangzhou—Deqing   / 210

Concluding Remarks

An Academic Journal Editor's Cultural Expression   / 216

目　录

第一章　华夏文明

华夏，中国也 .... /003

　　中文，世界文字史上唯一"活着"的语言 .... /007

中国文化名片 .... /011

　　秦始皇陵兵马俑 .... /013

　　万里长城 .... /015

　　祭祀天坛 .... /017

　　河姆渡文化遗址 .... /019

　　中国书画——"板桥"一绝 .... /021

　　中国戏曲——国粹京剧 .... /025

　　中国乐器 .... /027

　　中国陶瓷 .... /029

　　文化圣人——孔子 .... /031

第二章　神州大地

中国地理 .... /037

6

中国地图儿歌——《东方雄鸡图》 /041

中华民族大家庭 /045

大好河山 /047

母亲之河：长江、黄河 /047

奇山五岳：泰山雄、华山险、衡山秀、
恒山雅、嵩山峭 /049

高原西藏与布达拉宫 /051

明珠香港 /055

繁华澳门 /057

宝岛台湾 /059

其他省区市名称的故事 /061

第三章　中国古典文学集锦

《三国演义》 /087

《水浒传》 /089

《牡丹亭》 /091

第四章　中国古代建筑集锦

古塔楼阁 /095

六和塔   / 095

大雁塔   / 097

镇国塔   / 099

佑国寺塔   / 101

黄鹤楼   / 103

岳阳楼   / 103

滕王阁   / 105

蓬莱阁   / 105

江南水乡古镇   / 107

昆山周庄   / 107

吴江同里   / 107

桐乡乌镇   / 109

湖州南浔   / 109

吴中角直   / 111

嘉善西塘   / 111

第五章　中国民俗文化

中国节日（"年"）文化   / 115

春节和年　　　　　　　　　　　　　　　　/ 117

元宵节　　　　　　　　　　　　　　　　　/ 121

清明节　　　　　　　　　　　　　　　　　/ 123

端午节　　　　　　　　　　　　　　　　　/ 125

中秋节　　　　　　　　　　　　　　　　　/ 127

元　旦　　　　　　　　　　　　　　　　　/ 129

国际劳动节　　　　　　　　　　　　　　　/ 131

国际儿童节　　　　　　　　　　　　　　　/ 133

中华人民共和国国庆节　　　　　　　　　　/ 135

中国"吉祥"文化　　　　　　　　　　　　/ 137

福　　　　　　　　　　　　　　　　　　　/ 139

禄　　　　　　　　　　　　　　　　　　　/ 139

寿　　　　　　　　　　　　　　　　　　　/ 141

喜　　　　　　　　　　　　　　　　　　　/ 141

中华民俗——生肖文化　　　　　　　　　　/ 145

第六章　中华文苑

文房四宝——笔、墨、纸、砚　　　　　　　/ 153

中国书法——篆、隶、楷、行、草　　　　　　　　/ 155

中国书画四君子——梅、兰、竹、菊　　　　　　　/ 159

第七章　中国哲学

先秦时代的六大思想家　　　　　　　　　　　　　/ 169

　中国文化的先哲

　　　　——孔子（前551—前479）　　　　　　/ 173

　儒家理想主义流派代表

　　　　——孟子（约前371—前289）　　　　　/ 177

　儒家现实主义流派代表

　　　　——荀子（约前298—前238）　　　　　/ 179

　道家的创始人之一

　　　　——老子（约前571—前471）　　　　　/ 181

　道家早期最有影响的人物

　　　　——庄子（约前369—前286）　　　　　/ 183

　孔子的第一个反对者

　　　　——墨子（约前479—前381）　　　　　/ 185

第八章　现代中国一景：2008北京奥运

2008北京奥运会——中国奖牌亮点　　　　　　　　/ 191

北京奥运吉祥物——福娃的故事　　　　　　　　/ 199

第九章　家园之美——杭州

人间天堂——杭州　　　　　　　　　　　　　　/ 203

龙井茶香与陆羽的《茶经》　　　　　　　　　　/ 207

环绕杭州的水乡之美——德清　　　　　　　　　/ 211

后　记

一个学术期刊编辑的文化表达　　　　　　　　　/ 217

Chapter 1

The Civilization of China

华夏文明

HuaXia, China

In *The Grand Dictionary of the Chinese Language*, HuaXia (华夏) and China are synonymous. In fact, HuaXia is a bit similar to "Great Britain", because Hua signifies splendour and powerful civilization, and Xia will hark back to the beginning of Chinese civilization—Xia, Shang and Zhou times, among which Xia is the First Dynasty (c 2070–1600 BC), when ancient people claimed themselves as "HuaXia". As in the interpretation given by the Dictionary, ancient HuaXia tribes lived in the Yellow River Basin area that ranked as the world's centre where culture developed over a long period of time. As a result, the combination of two words "Hua" and "Xia" has the connotation of the national territory, and from ancient times to the present there has been the interpretation of HuaXia meaning China, and HuaXia civilization meaning the civilization of China.

It is well known that the place we call "China" has more than 3,000 years of recorded history. However, there was never a dynasty or a political power known as

© Zhejiang University Press 2016
Yuehong (Helen) Zhang, *Chinese Cultural Kaleidoscope*,
http://dx.doi.org/10.1631/ZUP.B978-7-308-15903-6_ch1

Made in 2003
制于二〇〇三年

华夏，中国也

　　"华夏"，《辞源》中解释为："夏，大也。故大国曰夏。华夏谓中国也。"若论内涵，该词类似于英国的"大不列颠（Great Britain）"含义。因为，"华"是一个形容词，意为华而贵，强而大。而"夏"则要追溯到中华文明史的开端，夏商周的时代。夏朝（约前2070—前1600）为中国历史上第一个朝代，那时起先民们已是自许为"华夏"。因古代的华夏族兴起于黄河流域，居四方之中，文明强大，历史悠久，故《辞源》中诠释为"华夏初指我国中原地区，后来包举我国全部领土而言"。于是乎，"华夏""中华"与"中国"皆为同义词。"华夏"两字的组合遂有了国家的内涵，自古至今也素有"华夏，中国也"的解读。

©浙江大学出版社 2016

张月红，《中国文化万花筒》，

http://dx.doi.org/10.1631/ZUP.B978-7-308-15903-6_ch1

"China" as the country name until the Xinhai Revolution and it has been a glory sign rooted in the hearts of generations of Chinese, which not only is derived from geography, but also is an historical symbol of a cultural standard. From Xia, Shang, Zhou to the end of the Qing Dynasty, there are countless changes from dynasties to regimes. After the Revolution, on New Year's Day 1912, the founding of Zhonghua Minguo (the Chinese Republic), Zhongguo (China), was adopted as the abbreviation. In 1949, with the founding of the People's Republic of China, "Zhongguo", China, as a country name acquired a whole new meaning.[1]

---

[1] The above brief introduction about the names of China is based on a reference by *The Grand Dictionary of the Chinese Language* published in the Commercial Press in 1983, and R. Wang's *A Panorama of China* published by Shanghai Foreign Language Education Press, 2011.

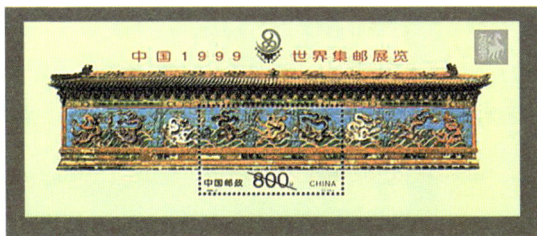

　　"中国"一词的考证约有三千年的文字记载，但之前仅是一个世代根植于中华民族心灵深处，由地域衍生，又具文化本位的一个历史性的象征符号。从夏商周起一直至清末，政权更替，朝代递嬗，几不可胜数，却从来没有一个王朝或政权曾以"中国"作为正式国名。直至辛亥革命以后，1912 年的元旦，中华民国成立，国际上称为"Republic of China"，简称 China（中国——Zhongguo）。至此，"中国"一名才成为有近代国家概念的正式名词。1949 年中华人民共和国成立，将中国概念完善到今天的含义。[1]

---

[1] 以上内容参阅了 1983 年商务印书馆的《辞源》与 2010 年上海外语教育出版社出版的汪榕培的《全景中国》等。

The Background to Chinese Characters—The sole survivors of the world's oldest four writing systems

China, an ancient civilization with thousands of years of continuous history, has left many cultural relics. Archaeological excavations have revealed not only that China is one of the world's oldest civilizations, but also that "the Chinese have created the single most extensive and enduring civilization in the world. Their language, spoken and written in the same forms over nearly four thousand years, binds their vast country together and links the present with the past, expressing a unified culture unmatched elsewhere", as described in the introduction provided at the British Museum. This is not only a miracle of the history of world writing systems, but also a key factor in Chinese civilization.

Actually, as a Chinese, when you stand in the National Museum of Chinese Writing in Anyang, Henan Province, you will be so proud of Chinese characters, especially because this is the only "living language"

中文，世界文字史上唯一"活着"的语言

中国是世界文明古国之一。悠悠历史长河沉淀了诸多的文化遗迹。众多的考古发掘证明中华民族是最先步入文明社会的民族之一。亦如大英博物馆的介绍中描述的，"中国人创造了一个世界上最广泛和持久的文明，正如他们的语言文字，在近四千年的历史中其口语与书面形式相同，将其庞大的国家凝聚在一起，连着过去和现在，表达着一统的文化，这是其他地方无法比拟的文化力量"。

surviving from ancient times to today in the history of human civilization. As the historical witness of that in the history of world civilization, there have only been a few instances of the creation of writing systems, such as the "Sumerian Cuneiform Script in Western Asia (西亚苏美尔的楔形文字), Hieroglyphics in Egypt (埃及的象形文字) and the Harappan Script of India (印度的哈拉帕文字), and Chinese Oracle-Bone inscription (中国的甲骨文字) as four great ancient scripts". They are all important signposts of early civilization. However, the first three scripts have disappeared for various reasons. Only Chinese characters, because of their spirit of changing with the times and tolerating differences, still exist in today's world as the Museum describes in its preface.

In short, Chinese characters are the sole survivors in the history of world civilization of several ancient writing systems.

　　的确，身为中国人，当您身处河南安阳"中国文字博物馆"时，面对人类文明史上唯一"活着"的中华文字时，那种骄傲是炎黄子孙的自得。事实上，人类考古已经见证，世界文明史中曾经"出现过几种独特古老的表意文字痕迹，如西亚的楔形文字、埃及的象形文字、印度的哈拉帕文字与中国的甲骨文字，为世界最早的四大古文字。它们均为人类早期文明的重要标志，但是由于种种原因其他三种已经被历史湮没，唯有中华汉字以其独有的魅力与时共进地传承至今"。这在世界文明史上不能不说是个奇迹，也是中华文明的福音！

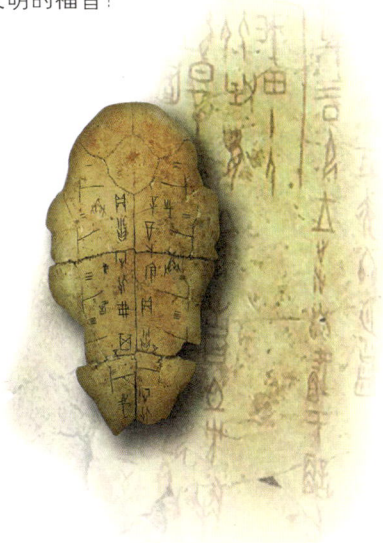

Chinese Culture Cards

"China is not only one of the world's oldest civilizations, but also the Chinese have created the single most extensive and enduring civilization in the world", as it says in the introduction provided at the British Museum. Here we cite a few famous "Chinese Culture Cards" to provide a guide for our readers all over the world. Of course, the following topic section will make you more fascinated!

中国文化名片

正如大英博物馆对中国馆的导读词中所述："中华民族创造了一个世界上最广泛和持久的文明……"这里不妨信手呈上世人皆知的几爿中国文化名片做个导读吧。当然，后面的章节会依主题展示，让读者对中华文化名片的魅力更是着迷。

The Terracotta Warriors of the Qin Dynasty

The year 1974 witnessed a sensational archaeological find of brown pottery fragments of life-like sized terracotta warriors and horses in Xi'an, once the capital of thirteen Chinese dynasties. These warriors represent a microcosm of life during the Qin Dynasty (221–207 BC) and give insight into the history of both Chinese art and war tactics. Being the most significant archeological excavation of the 20th century, it is renowned as the eighth wonder of the world.

秦始皇陵兵马俑

1974 年，在曾经为 13 朝故都的西安，秦始皇陵兵马俑坑的发现震惊了世界。这一建在公元前 3 世纪的地下雕塑群，以恢弘磅礴的气势、威武严整的军阵、形态逼真的陶俑，向人们展示古代东方文化的灿烂辉煌。其无论建造年代、建筑规模还是艺术效果，无不堪与"世界七大奇迹"媲美，被誉为"世界第八大奇迹"。

The Great Wall

Historical records trace the construction of the original Great Wall defensive fortification back to the year 656 BC. After over 2,000 years of rebuilding, the Wall now stretches westward for 21,196 kilometers, and so is known as the Ten-Thousand-Li Wall in China. It is not only a rare and massive piece of architecture, but also the urban or rural environment that witnessed certain civilizations, significant social developments or historical events. That is why it continues to be so attractive to people all over the world. Like the Pyramids of Egypt, the Taj Mahal in India and the Hanging Gardens of Babylon, it is credited as one of the great wonders of the world.

万里长城

　　长城始建于春秋战国时期，历时达 2000 多年，总长度达 21,196 千米以上。雄伟壮观的万里长城是人类建筑史上罕见的古代军事防御工程，是中华民族的骄傲与象征，凝聚着我们祖先的血汗和智慧。它以悠久的历史、浩大的工程、雄伟的气魄著称于世。它早就和埃及的金字塔、印度的泰姬陵、伊斯坦布尔的圣•索菲亚教堂等一起被誉为世界的奇迹。

The Temple of Heaven

The Temple of Heaven in southern Beijing, built in 1420, the 18th year of the reign of the Ming Emperor Yongle, was where emperors went to worship Heaven for good harvests. With an area of 2.7 million square meters, it is the largest of its kind in China. It is distinguished over the world for its distinctive layout, unique architecture and magnificent decoration. As a cultural heritage, it belongs not only to China but to the world as well.

祭祀天坛

　　天坛位于北京天安门的东南。始建于明永乐十八年（1420），原名"天地坛"，是明清两代皇帝祭祀天地之神的地方。天坛共占地270万平方米，规模宏伟，富丽堂皇，是中国现存最大的古代祭祀性建筑群。它以严谨的规划布局、奇特的建筑结构、瑰丽的建筑装饰著称于世。它不仅在中国建筑史上占有重要位置，也是世界建筑艺术的珍贵遗产。

Hemudu Culture Site

The 7,000-year-old Hemudu Cultural Site located in Zhejiang Province, southern China, is an important Stone Age cultural site and representative of historical and cultural sites in the Yangtze River area.

河姆渡文化遗址

我们身边的河姆渡文化遗址，距今已有 7000 多年的历史，位于浙江省境内，地处中国的南部。这是新石器时代的重要文化遗址，也是长江流域文化遗址的重要代表。

Painting & Calligraphy—Works by Zheng Banqiao

Zheng Banqiao (AD 1693–1765) was an ancient Chinese calligraphy and painter, good at bamboo, stone and orchids (see the stamps). His interesting paintings reveal power and elegance. His calligraphy was very unique and looked like riprap paving. His many excellent works were handed down from ancient times and, in addition to his paintings, his calligraphy works are also very good. In particular his handwriting means in English, "Where ignorance is bliss, it is folly to be wise". This phrase has become a marvellous quotation since 1751.

The splendid achievements of Chinese calligraphy and painting are the best manifestations of the profound Chinese culture. The masters of Chinese calligraphy and painting are like oysters cultivating pearls. With persevering patience, they contributed greatly to the development and propagation of Chinese calligraphy and painting. Writing brushes, paper, inkstick and inkstone are four necessary treasures for creating traditional Chinese

中国书画——"板桥"一绝

在中华文明史上，中国书画担当了华夏文明的传承与载体。而"中国书画"这一术语，意含中国书法与中国绘画，两者相辅相成，合二为一。自有了笔墨纸砚传情写意以来，历朝历代的中国书画家以其辉煌夺目的成

calligraphy and paintings reflecting Chinese history and culture. In the chapters that follow, there are some more interesting samples for your information.

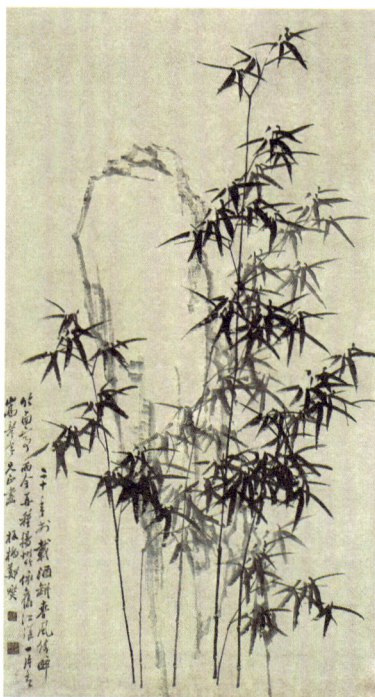

就，为中华文化的博大精深做了无与伦比的诠释，也留下了书家画人的才情浪漫，及千古传世的杰作与墨宝。令现代人不觉回目感叹，在中国几千年的书画史上，有多少千古名流沉睡？！

今天，我们选了清朝时期的著名书画大家郑板桥（1693—1765）一展趣味。他名为郑燮，人称"板桥先生"。一生主居扬州，以卖画为生，尤其以画竹、石、兰而出神入化，妙趣横生，自成体系，可谓中国古代书画家中一绝。更绝的是他的书法题词"难得糊涂"已是世代公认的"传世名言"，不仅写法具"板桥"型，而且四个字透出了做人的"大智慧"，被世人叫绝！

Beijing Opera

Traditional Chinese opera has a very long history. Among many styles of opera still existing, the most influential one is Beijing Opera, regarded as the quintessence of China. This special artistic form is very popular in foreign countries, and has become a stepping stone for communication between Chinese and foreign cultures.

中国戏曲——国粹京剧

　　中国的戏曲艺术历史悠远，发展到今天已有数百戏种，其中影响最为深远的当数京剧。其腔调以西皮、二黄为主，用胡琴和锣鼓等伴奏，分布以北京为中心，遍及全国。京剧在清朝宫廷内很快时兴，到民国时期空前繁荣。同时，京剧这种特有的艺术形式走出国门后，被视为中国国粹而深受各界人士的欢迎，成为传播中国传统文化艺术的重要媒介。

Ancient musical instruments

Traditional Chinese musical instruments can be mainly classified into three categories: string, wind and percussion. Their representative instruments are the Xun, Xiao, Sheng, Pipa, Guqin, Drum, Dizi, and Chinese Chimes, among which the most ancient Chinese musical instrument is the Xun, an egg-shaped 6-holes porcelain wind instrument developed in the Shang and Zhou dynasties. The Xun is full of the special charm of that period, with its special features of primitive simplicity, vigor, gloom, vicissitude, mystery and sadness. The Xun is good at expressing pathetic feelings, and solemn, remote and sad effects, and has always been regarded as a special musical instrument.

中国乐器

中国乐器是华夏文明史上的文化名片之一。古时，声音是一种绝美的享受。根据《周礼》所述，乐器依材质分为：金（钟）、石（磬）、丝（琴瑟）、竹（管箫）、匏（笙）、土（埙）、革（鼓）、木（笛），素称为"八音"。其代表乐器分别为编钟、磬、瑟、萧、笙、埙、鼓、笛。它们当中，埙约有七千年的历史，是当之无愧最古老的中国乐器。随着考古和对古乐器复原工作研究的进展，相信身边的、民族的就是世界的，人们会对中国乐器演奏的乐章深深着迷。

Chinese pottery

Potter's clay is the source of porcelain and porcelain utensils evolved from clay pottery. Clay pottery and porcelain utensils, with their long history, were the starting points of ancient Chinese culture as early as 7,000 years ago. Potter's clay, after molding and heating from a 500–600°C flame, becomes clay pottery usually used as water containers. Porcelain vases, after molding and heating from a 1200–1300°C flame, are usually for holding flowers. They are very beautiful and elegant. The evolution from clay pottery to porcelain utensils indicates the progress of human civilization.

中国陶瓷

中国瓷器的发明是对世界文明的一大贡献，瓷器的故乡在中国。早在7000多年前，华夏的先祖们就已经制造和使用陶器了。陶土经过500~600℃的窑火煅烧制成的陶罐多用于生活。的确，陶是瓷的源，瓷是陶的流。瓷土要经过1200~1300℃的窑火才能烧成瓷器，除了作为生活用品，还有了观赏的价值。从陶到瓷的变化是人类文明的进步。而世界也是最早从瓷器（china）认识了中国。

Chinese culture's wise man—Confucius

The doctrines of Confucius and his disciples especially stress the practice and cultivation of filial piety, benevolence, righteousness, wisdom and loyalty. After development for several thousand years, the doctrines have become the basis for most theories of ethics, education, politics and religion in China.

Confucius (551–479 BC) has a formal given name, Qiu, and styled himself Zhongni. He hailed from the Zou State of Lu (now the southeast part of Qufu City in Shandong) at the end of the Spring-Autumn Period. He was a famous ideologist, educator and initiator of Confucianism in ancient China. It was said that he had

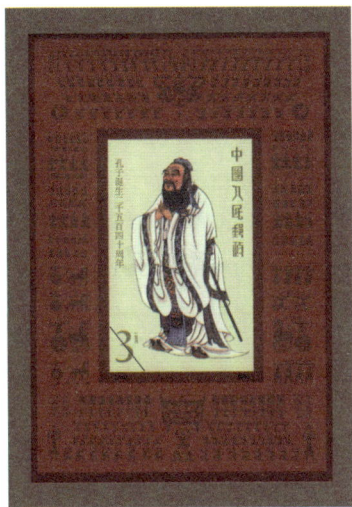

文化圣人——孔子

　　中国文化深受孔子儒家思想的影响。2000 多年来，世代的华夏子民奉孔子为文化圣人，拜孔子为教育第一师长，视孔子为最伟大的古代哲学思想家。简言之，孔子就是中华文化思想的集大成者。中华民族永远会因孔子诞生

three thousand disciples, and seventy-two of the best ones in literary works. He edited *The Book of Songs* and *Collection of Ancient Texts*, finalized *The Rites* and *The Music*, wrote the preface to *The Books of Changes in the Zhou Dynasty* and wrote *The Spring and Autumn Annals*. His thoughts and doctrines have a profound influence in China even long after his lifetime. In a following chapter (Chapter 7), his philosophy will be introduced in detail.

于华夏大地而骄傲，世界也因孔子而对博大精深的中国文化惊叹不已。这就是孔子在中华文化史上的名片魅力。

出生在春秋末年鲁国陬邑（山东曲阜）的孔子（前551—前479），名丘，字仲尼。一生刻苦好学，中年时开办私学，周游列国，相传有弟子三千追随，其中传说有七十二贤弟子也成为当时著名学者而青史留名。同时，孔子也是古代第一位文献编撰者，传说他编《诗》《书》《礼》《乐》，序《周易》，作《春秋》。一言以蔽之，孔子的思想及著作，以及他所处的文化繁荣的春秋战国时代，对后世乃至世界文化都产生了不朽的影响。

Chapter 2

The Land of China
神州大地

Geography of China

China is located in Eastern Asia, to the west of the Pacific Ocean (see Fig. 2 Map of the People's Republic of China. Detailed Map on the inside front cover of this book). The land of China is one of great geographical diversity, high in the west and low in the east, its mountains, plateaux and hills accounting for about 67% and the basin and plain for about 33%. Bordered by mountains, steppes and deserts, the immense central plains and plateaux are watered by great rivers, such as the Yellow and Yangtze Rivers, supporting a dense population, about 1,37 billion.

Its vast territory, with a total area of about 9.6 million square kilometers, over 5,000 km in distance from east to west, a coastline of over 18,000 km, makes it second only to Russia and Canada, ranking No. 3 in the world (the fourth being the United States), with an area almost equivalent to the whole of Europe.

China has 23 provinces (ANHUI, FUJIAN, GANSU, GUANGDONG, GUIZHOU, HEBEI, HENAN, HEILONGJIANG,

© Zhejiang University Press 2016

Yuehong (Helen) Zhang, *Chinese Cultural Kaleidoscope*,

http://dx.doi.org/10.1631/ZUP.B978-7-308-15903-6_ch2

Fig. 1　Map of the People's Republic of China
图1　中华人民共和国地图（详图见封二）

中国地理

    中国位于亚洲东部、太平洋的西岸（中国地图见图1，详图见封二）。其地域辽阔，群山环绕，西高东低，山地、高原和丘陵约占陆地面积的67%，盆地和平原约占陆地面积的33%。国土面积约960万平方千米，东西相距约5000千米，大陆海岸线长达18000多千米。其面积仅次于俄罗斯和加拿大，居世界第三位，几乎等同于整个欧洲

© 浙江大学出版社 2016
张月红，《中国文化万花筒》，
http://dx.doi.org/10.1631/ZUP.B978-7-308-15903-6_ch2

HUNAN, HUBEI, JILIN, JIANGXI, JIANGSU, LIAONING, SHANDONG, SHAANXI, SHANXI, SICHUAN, YUNNAN, ZHEJIANG, QINGHAI, HAINAN, and TAIWAN); five autonomous regions (GUANGXI, INNER MONGOLIA, NINGXIA, TIBET, XINJIANG); two special administrative regions (HONG KONG and MACAO); and four municipalities directly under the central government (BEIJING, SHANGHAI, TIANJIN and CHONGQING). The capital city of China is Beijing.

的面积。

　　中国的省级行政区总共有 34 个。其中有 23 个省（安徽、福建、甘肃、广东、贵州、河北、河南、黑龙江、湖南、湖北、吉林、江西、江苏、辽宁、山东、陕西、山西、四川、云南、浙江、青海、海南和台湾），5 个自治区（广西壮族自治区、内蒙古自治区、宁夏回族自治区、西藏自治区和新疆维吾尔自治区），2 个特别行政区（香港与澳门）和 4 个直辖市（北京、天津、上海和重庆）。首都为北京。

　　在这广袤的中华土地上，伟大的母亲河——黄河和长江养育着 13 亿多的中华儿女。

Yamdrok Lake by YL Fang
羊湖（方宇珑摄）

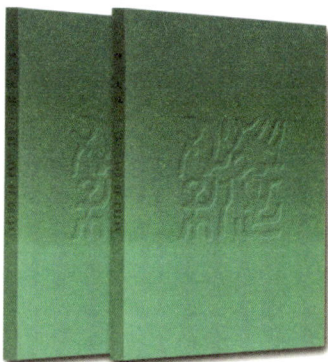

Made in 2003
制于二〇〇三年

Children's folk song—Chinese Rooster Map

The main inhabited areas of the Chinese nation are based on the topographical maps of China. According to the earliest geographical books in Chinese, such as *The Classics of Mountains and Oceans* (*Shan Hai Ching*), its geographic outline is very similar to that of a cockerel, or rooster. There is also a children's folk song which says that the Chinese rooster shape can be used to describe the following:

中国地图儿歌——《东方雄鸡图》

中华民族主要聚居地的中国版图，据说早年先秦古籍的地理著作——《山海经》中有所描述。由此，民间一直流传着一首孩子们口口相传的地图儿歌，即《东方雄鸡图》。歌词唱到"中国地图像雄鸡，昂首挺胸真神气……"，这里我们不妨快乐地唱一唱：

China's map looks like a rooster

（雄鸡图：拍摄自杭州城站火车站广告画）

Children's folk song—Chinese Rooster Map

*China's map looks like a rooster, in which really good
    songs come from the rooster with its head held
    high and chest puffed out.*

*The Yellow River is China's Mother River and is more like
    the rooster's arteries that lead to its heart.*

*The northeast's three provinces are located in the
    head of the rooster, which are Jilin, Liaoning and
    Heilongjiang.*

*Gansu and Inner Mongolia are located on the back of
    the rooster and the rooster's tail is Xinjiang and
    Tibet.*

*Yunnan, Guangxi and Hainan are similar to the rooster's
    legs and feet.*

Guangdong and Fujian are the chest of the rooster.

*Zhejiang and Jiangsu are the rooster's breast, and
    Shandong and Hebei are the rooster's neck.*

Taiwan is surrounded by the East China Sea.

(Here, please remember 1997 and 1999,

When Hong Kong and Macao returned to our motherland[1].)

*Tianjing surrounds the rooster's breast, protecting the
    capital city of Beijing.*

*(The other two municipalities directly under the Central
    Government are Shanghai and Chongqing.)*

*In this way, when the children look at the map, they can
    remember the parts of the rooster to clearly know
    the different areas of China.*

---

[1] It is a very early ballad. However, in 1997 and 1999 Hong Kong and Macao returned
    to our motherland, so the author made a few changes here.

中国地图儿歌——《东方雄鸡图》

黄河是中国的母亲河，
更像是雄鸡心脏的大动脉。
中国地图像雄鸡，
昂首挺胸真神气。
鸡头东北三个省，
辽宁、吉林、黑龙江。
鸡背甘肃、内蒙古，
鸡尾新疆和西藏。
云南、广西、海南岛，
就像雄鸡的腿和脚。
广东、福建是鸡脯，
浙江、江苏是鸡胸。
山东、河北是鸡颈，
台湾围在东海中。
(孩子们，还要记住 1997 和 1999
香港、澳门回家了。)[1]
天津守在鸡胸口，
保卫首都北京城。
(另外两个直辖市是上海和重庆。)
小朋友们看地图，
祖国地名记得清。

---

[1] 1997年与1999年，是香港和澳门分别回归中国，成为两个特别行政区的年
　份，括号里的相关内容是作者对这首早年民谣《东方雄鸡图》的改动。

Chinese People's Family

During the long 5,000-year history, in our homeland of over 9.6 million square kilometers, the Han nationality, the main part of our population, together with another 55 minorities, like the Zhuang, Mongolian, Hui, Tibetan, Uygur, Miao, Tujia, Yi, Buyi, Korean, Manchu, Dong, Yao, Bai, Gaoshan, Naxi minorities, etc., have been merged into a great Chinese People's family with characteristic Chinese culture (see the stamp).

中华民族大家庭

960 万平方千米的土地上，在五千年的历史长河中，以汉族为主体的 56 个民族互相融合成为伟大的中华民族。中华民族共同创造了光辉灿烂的华夏文化。中华民族中汉族人口占绝大部分，人口在 100 万以上的少数民族有壮族、蒙古族、回族、藏族、维吾尔族、苗族、土家族、彝族、布依族、朝鲜族、满族、侗族、瑶族和白族等，人口较少的有赫哲族和珞巴族等。

Our Beloved Motherland
Yellow and Yangtze rivers—mother rivers

In the long history of the Chinese nation, the Yangtze River (6,380 kilometers) and Yellow River (5,464 kilometers), Chinese mother rivers, gave birth to the great Chinese civilization. The Three Gorges of the Yangtze River extend 205 kilometers from the western Baidi City to the Nanjinguan Pass in the east.

For Baidi City, as the greatest romantic poet of the Tang Dynasty, Li Bai (AD 701–762), described in his widely known poem, "Baidi City I left at dawn in the morning-glow of the clouds; the thousand *li* to Jiangling, we sailed in a single day. On either shore the gibbons' chatter sounded without pause, while my light boat skimmed past a thousand mountains."

The Yangtze River is the longest river in China and also the origin of the splendid Chinese culture. Currently the world-famous Three Gorges Power Project has already been erected on the scenic Yangtze River.

大好河山

母亲之河：长江、黄河

在中华民族历史的长河上，长江（总长6380千米）和黄河（总长5464千米）孕育了灿烂的中华文明。而三峡又是长江的珠冠，它西起重庆奉节的白帝城，东到湖北宜昌的南津关，总长205千米。这里山势雄奇险峻，江流奔腾湍急，峡区礁滩接踵，夹岸峰插云天，是闻名遐迩的游览胜地。唐朝浪漫主义诗人李白(701—762)《早发白帝城》一诗，"朝辞白帝彩云间，千里江陵一日还。两岸猿声啼不住，轻舟已过万重山"，淋漓尽致地描写了长江的壮观。今天，以风景闻名于世的三峡又以一个跨世纪的全球超级工程而举世瞩目——一个具有防洪、发电和航运等功能的巨大的长江三峡工程在此落地，千古奇迹任后人评说感慨。

The five sacred mountains in China

China is famous for its beautiful mountains, among which the five sacred mountains are the most distinguished. They are: East Mountain, Mount Tai in Shandong Province, famous for its magnificence; West Mountain, Mount Hua in Shaanxi Province, especially famous for its awe-inspiring grandeur; South Mountain, Mount Heng in Hunan Province, well-known for its elegance; Mount Heng in Shanxi Province, the northern one and also the peaceful and pure one; Middle Mountain, Mount Song located in Henan Province, well known for its steep cliffs and holy Taoism site. All are prized for their individuality and expressiveness. In history they were ancient China's political, economic and cultural centres. Take Mount Tai as an example: There were in total 72 emperors from the Xia, Shang and Zhou dynasties who built temples on it. And from the Qin to Qing Dynasty, according to the historical records, there were 12 emperors offering their worship on sacred Mount Tai.

奇山五岳：
泰山雄、华山险、衡山秀、恒山雅、嵩山峭

　　中华大地名山众多，其中以五岳最为有名，有"五岳归来不看山"之誉。它们分别是：东岳泰山，位于山东，以雄伟出名；西岳华山，位于陕西，以险著称；南岳衡山，位于湖南，钟灵毓秀；北岳恒山，位于山西，幽静淡雅；中岳嵩山，位于河南，峻峭挺拔，亦为道教圣地。古代封建帝王把五岳看成是神的象征，常来拜祭，如泰山，相传上古时期就有 72 代君王曾封禅泰山。自秦至清，史籍上确切记载曾来到泰山封禅祭祀的皇帝共有 12 位。

Tibet and its Potala Palace

"Tibet" comes from "Stod-bod", which was the old name before the Ming Dynasty. The Tibet region was called "Dbus-Gtsang" in the Yuan and Ming dynasties. "Dbus" means "centre" in the Tibetan language, and "Gtsang" means "holiness". As situated in the west of China, it is called "Xizang" (which means "Western Zang") in Chinese. The Tibet Autonomous Region was established in 1965, with the abbreviation of "藏" (Zang). Its capital is Lhasa.

Reclining against and capping the Red Hill in the northwest of Lhasa, the world famous monastery-like palace, the Potala Palace, more than 3,700 metres

高原西藏与布达拉宫

元朝、明朝称西藏地区为乌斯藏，“乌斯”是藏语“中央”的意思，藏是“圣洁”的意思。因为它在中国西部，称西藏。1965 年成立西藏自治区，简称藏。自治区的首府是拉萨市。

Tibetan Prayer by JF Zhang
虔诚的藏民（张剑锋摄）

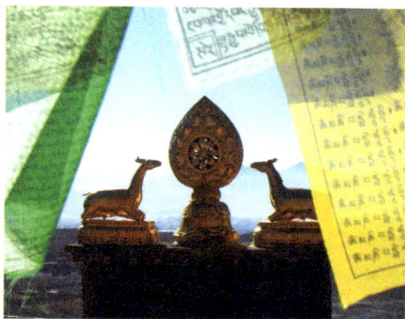

Statues of Deer Listening to Sutras by YL Fang
双鹿听经（方宇珑摄）

above sea level, covering a total area of 360,000 square meters, was the religious and political centre of old Tibet and the winter palace of the Dalai Lamas. The palace is more than 117 meters high, 360 metres wide, and has thirteen floors, occupying a building space of 130,000 square meters. It is composed of the White Palace and Red Palace for secular use and religious use, respectively. Consisting of various palaces, chambers, a Buddhist official seminary, hallways, murals, country yards, Dharma Cave and the Saint's Chapel, Potala is one of the grandest palaces in the world.

举世闻名的布达拉宫就位于拉萨市西北的玛布日山（红山），是我国著名的宫堡式建筑群，是藏族古建筑艺术的精华。布达拉宫以其辉煌的雄姿和藏传佛教圣地的地位，成为举世公认的藏民族的象征，一直作为西藏政治和宗教的中心。布达拉宫海拔3700多米，占地总面积36万余平方米，建筑总面积13万余平方米，主楼高117米，宽360米，共13层，全部为石木结构。其中宫殿、灵塔殿、佛殿、经堂、僧舍和庭院等一应俱全，是当今世界上海拔最高、规模最大的宫殿式建筑群。

The Potala Palace by JF Zhang
雨中布达拉宫（张剑锋摄）

Hong Kong

Hong Kong is a special administrative region of China and an international free trade port. Hong Kong, the Harbor of Fragrance, is a crowded, prosperous, international metropolis, also a charming place, a paradise for tourists. Here, visitors can experience the fun of sightseeing and shopping and enjoy delicious food and fine entertainment. The exchange and mutual fusion of cultures have also made Hong Kong unique as a place where East meets West and ancient culture merges with modern culture.

明珠香港

香港（Hong Kong），1997年回归祖国，其作为一个特别行政区和国际自由贸易港，早已是举世闻名的动感之都，享有"东方之珠"的美誉，也是一个生活的乐园，集各式各样的欢乐于一地。在香港旅游，游客既可以观赏到美丽的自然风光，又可以享受商业文明带来的种种快乐；同样还可以重温体味旧时的朴真生活。

Macau

Macau was returned to China and became a special administrative region of China on December 20th, 1999. It has a unique natural and cultural attraction, with showplaces, ancient or foreign structures. Buildings and alleyways have all become witness to the past of Macau. Its busiest commercial area is the place near the city hall, where the Ruins of St.Paul's stand as the symbol of Macau.

繁华澳门

澳门特别行政区（Macau）1999 年回归祖国，有着独特的人文和自然景观，成为中西方文化的交融之处。澳门众多的名胜古迹、中外建筑及街区小巷，都成为凝固的文化，散发着其特有的迷人气息，成为澳门历经数百年风雨的见证。澳门的繁华地段集中在市政厅一带，其中圣保罗教堂的牌坊已成为澳门的象征。

Taiwan

Being China's biggest island, with a total area of about 36,000 square kilometers, Taiwan includes 64 islands previously known as the Penghu Islands and 21 other islands. Shaped roughly like a tobacco leaf, Taiwan is 394 kilometers long and 144 kilometers wide at its broadest point. Situated in the Pacific Ocean about 160 kilometers from the southeastern coast of the Chinese mainland and with the Philippines to the south, Taiwan is a natural gateway for travellers to and within Asia.

In history, there were various names for the Taiwan Province: Yizhou, Liuqiu, Dongfan, Beigang, Dayuan, Dawan, and Taiwan. In the reign of Emperor Guangxu, the Qing government formally made Taiwan a province, and "Tai" as the abbreviation.

宝岛台湾

台湾位于我国东南海域，东临太平洋，西隔台湾海峡与福建相望，南靠巴士海峡与菲律宾群岛相对，北向东海。台湾总面积约36000平方千米，本岛呈纺锤形，南北纵长约394千米，东西宽约144千米。台湾由台湾本岛及兰屿、绿岛、钓鱼岛等21个附属岛屿和澎湖列岛64个岛屿构成，是中国最大的岛屿，故台湾被称为"多岛之省"。台湾海峡为中国南北方之间的海上交通要道，亦是著名的远东海上走廊。

中国古代历史上台湾曾被称为"夷州"，或"流求"，又称"东番""大员"及"大湾"等，后又改为台湾。清光绪年间建台湾省，简称台。

The origins of geographical names of the other provinces, cities and regions

Beijing City

Beijing was known as "Ji" in the Warring States Period, being the capital of Yan which was one of the seven Warring States. It was named "Yanjing" by Liao, "Jingdu" in the Jin Dynasty, and "Dadu" in the Yuan Dynasty. Zhu Yuanzhang (Ming Dynasty) then changed it to "Beiping", and later the Yongle Emperor (Zhu Di) further changed it to "Beijing". The one-character abbreviation is "Jing". Since 1949, Beijing has been the capital of the People's Republic of China.

Tianjin City

In the Ming Dynasty, the Prince of Yan launched a war against the Jianwen Emperor (his nephew) and defeated him. In memory of the rising here at the river crossing, it was named "Tianjin", meaning "a Port for the Emperor". The one-character abbreviation is "Jin". Tianjin has been one of four municipalities directly under the central government since 1967 (including AD 1949–1958).

其他省区市名称的故事[1]

北京市

战国时期称蓟，是"战国七雄"之一燕国的京城。辽国称燕京。金国改称京都。元朝称大都。明朝朱元璋改称北平，永乐帝朱棣改北平为北京，简称京。自1949年中华人民共和国成立后，北京是中国的首都。

天津市

明朝，燕王为争夺皇帝之位，在这里发兵渡河南下，打败他的侄子明惠帝而篡了位。为纪念在这里渡河起兵，所以称"天津"，意即天子经过的渡口，简称津。自1967年至今（之前包括1949—1958年间）为中国的4个直辖市之一。

---

[1] 这部分中文资料主要参考百度文库的"中国各省区名字的由来"。

Shanghai City

In the early Northern Song Dynasty, Shanghai had become one of the settlements. People put out to sea from here, and thus it was named "Shanghai". It was originally a place for fishing. Fishermen developed fishing gear named "Yong" which was made of bamboo, sticking up in the water. Later "Yong" was changed to "Hu", which is now the one-character abbreviation of Shanghai. Shanghai has been one of four municipalities directly under the central government since 1949.

Chongqing City

Chongqing city was called "Ba" in ancient times. It was called "Jiangzhou" in the Qin Dynasty, "Gongzhou" in the Northern Song Dynasty. The name of "Chongqing" dated back to 1190, since the Emperor Guangzong of the Southern Song Dynasty was first granted the title "Prince Gong" here and then inherited the throne, raising "Gongzhou" to "Chongqing Fu" and claiming "double happiness". In the Sui Dynasty, Jialing River was called "Yushui". Since Chongqing is sited by the Jialing River and located at Yuzhou, the one-character abbreviation is thus "Yu". Since 1997, Chongqing

上海市

北宋初期，这里已形成居民点，从这里"上"海入洋，所以称上海。上海原来是捕鱼的地方，当时渔民创造了一种捕鱼工具，叫"邕"（它是由竹子编成，插在水中），后来邕改为沪，所以上海简称沪。自 1949 年始，上海市一直是中国 4 个直辖市之一。

重庆市

重庆古称"巴"，秦时称江州，隋称渝州，北宋称恭州。重庆之名始于 1190 年，因南宋光宗赵敦先封恭王，后登帝位，遂将恭州升为重庆府，取"双重喜庆"之意。隋时，嘉陵江称渝水，重庆因位于嘉陵江畔而置渝州，故重庆简称"渝"。1997 年始，重庆成为中国 4 个直辖市之一。

has been one of four municipalities directly under the central government, too.

Heilongjiang Province

The name of Heilongjiang Province is taken from the Black Dragon River ("Heilongjiang" in Chinese). The river is coloured dark green, meandering like a swimming dragon. The name of Heilongjiang Province dates back to 1907. The one-character abbreviation is "Hei". Its capital is Harbin.

Jilin Province

In the Qing Dynasty, Wula City in Jilin (today's Jilin City) had been founded along the Songhua River. In Manchu "Jilin" means "along" and "Wula" "great rivers"; together it means a city on the Songhua River. The name of Jilin Province had been used when it was founded. The one-character abbreviation is "Ji". Its capital is Changchun.

Liaoning Province

It is located in the Liao River basin, meaning "permanent peace". The name of Liaoning Province dates back to 1929. The one-character abbreviation is "Liao". Its capital is Shenyang.

黑龙江省

由黑龙江而得名。因为江水呈黑绿色，蜿蜒地流着像条游龙。简称黑。1907年设置黑龙江省。省会是哈尔滨市。

吉林省

清朝在松花江沿岸建立吉林乌拉城（今吉林市），满语吉林是"沿"的意思，乌拉是"大川"的意思，合起来就是沿着松花江的城市。后来建省时，就用它命名叫吉林省。简称吉。省会是长春市。

辽宁省

由于它在辽河流域，1929年取辽河永久安宁之意，设置辽宁省。简称辽。省会是沈阳市。

Hebei Province

It is located to the north of the Yellow River. In the Tang Dynasty, "Hebei Road" referred to the district which was to the north of the Yellow River and to the east of the Taihang Mountains. The name of Hebei Province dates back to 1928. The one-character abbreviation is "Ji" because it belonged to Jizhou in ancient China. Its capital is Shijiazhuang.

Henan Province

It is mostly to the south of the Yellow River. Belonging to Yuzhou in ancient times, it is called "Yu" for short. It has been a province since the Ming Dynasty. Its capital is Zhengzhou.

Shanxi Province

It is to the west of the Taihang Mountain. It has been a province since the Ming Dynasty. During the Spring-Autumn Period it belonged to Jin State, so it is called "Jin" for short. Its capital is Taiyuan.

Shandong Province

It is to the east of the Taihang Mountain. It has been a province since the Ming Dynasty. During the Spring-

河北省

相对于黄河为北。唐朝时黄河以北、太行山以东地区为河北道，1928 年称河北省。因古代属冀州地区，所以简称冀。省会是石家庄市。

河南省

相对于黄河为南。主要部分在黄河以南，因为古代属豫州地区，所以简称豫。明初设置河南省。省会是郑州市。

山西省

相对于太行山为西。明朝设置山西省，春秋时是晋国领土，所以简称晋。省会是太原市。

Autumn Period it belonged to Lu State, so it is called "Lu" for short. Its capital is Jinan.

Hunan Province

It is on the south side of Dongting Lake. The Xiangjiang River runs through the province, so it is called "Xiang" for short. It has been a province since the Qing Dynasty. Its capital is Changsha.

Hubei Province

It is located in the easternmost part of Central China. The province's name means "north of the lake", referring to its position north of Dongting Lake. The provincial capital was Wuchang in the Qing Dynasty, which belonged to Ezhou, so Hubei is officially abbreviated to "E". Its capital is Wuhan.

Zhejiang Province

It is located on the coastal sediment of the East China Sea, south of the Yangtze River Delta. The province's name derives from the Zhejiang River that is the former name of the Qiantang River, and is usually described as meaning "Crooked River" or "Bent River". Zhejiang Province is officially abbreviated to Zhe. It has been a province since

山东省

相对于太行山为东。明朝设置山东省，春秋时是鲁国领土，所以简称鲁。省会是济南市。

湖南省

相对于洞庭湖为南。由于湘江纵贯全省，所以简称湘。清代设置湖南省。省会是长沙市。

湖北省

位于中国中部偏南，长江中游，洞庭湖以北，故名湖北。由于清朝时省会武昌属于鄂州管辖，故简称鄂。省会是武汉市。

the Ming Dynasty. The provincial capital is Hangzhou.

Jiangxi Province

The name "Jiangxi" derived from the Circuit (Road) of Western Jiangnan administrated in the Tang dynasty, in Chinese, as Jiangnanxidao called "Jiangxidao" in short. It was renamed "Jiangxi Province" in the Qing Dynasty. The short name for Jiangxi Province is "Gan", due to the Gan River running through it from south to north and finally into the Yangtze River. This provincial capital is Nanchang.

Shaanxi Province

Shaanxi Province includes the region southwest of Shan County in Henan Province. The name "Shaanxi" means "land west of Shan", which is abbreviated to "Shan". For Shaanxi was the territory of the Qin Dynasty in ancient China, it is also abbreviated to "Qin". It has been a province since the Qing Dynasty. Its capital is Xi'an, an ancient and famous city.

Anhui Province

The name "Anhui" derives from the combination of the first Chinese characters of Anqing (now Anqing City) and Huizhou (now She County), two prefectures of

浙江省

地处中国东南沿海长江三角洲南翼，东临东海，南接福建，西与安徽、江西相连，北与上海、江苏接壤。境内最大的河流钱塘江，因江流曲折，称之江，又称浙江，故浙江省简称浙。明初设置浙江省。省会是杭州市。

江西省

唐朝为江南西道，简称江西道。清朝时改为江西省。因为赣江综贯全省，所以简称赣，省会是南昌市。

陕西省

简称"陕"，因为古代为秦国领地，又称为"秦"，清设置陕西省。省会是西安市。

the Qing Dynasty. The abbreviation for Anhui Province is "Wan", because of Mount Wan (also known as Mount Tianzhu) located in the province. Its capital is Hefei.

Jiangsu Province

The name "Jiangsu" comes from the combination of Jiangning (now Nanjing City) and Suzhou (now Suzhou City), two prefectures of the Qing Dynasty. The abbreviation for Jiangsu Province is "Su", the second character of its name. Its capital is Nanjing.

Gansu Province

Gansu Province, "Gan" for short, derives its name from the two ancient prefectures of Gan (now Zhangye City) and Su (now Jiuquan City). Liupan Mountain located in the province is also known as Long Mountain, and therefore Gansu Province is also called "Long" for short. It has been a province since the Qing Dynasty. Its capital is Lanzhou.

Guizhou Province

Guizhou was established as a province during the Ming Dynasty, which is abbreviated as "Gui". Historically, the area had belonged to Qianzhong County, so Guizhou Province is

安徽省

　　以清朝时的安庆府（今安庆市）和徽州府（今歙县）的头一字组成。因境内有皖山（天柱山），因而简称皖。省会是合肥市。

江苏省

　　是以清朝时的江宁府（今南京市）和苏州府（今苏州市）的头一个字组成。简称苏。省会是南京市。

甘肃省

　　是以古代甘州（今张掖）、肃州（今酒泉）的头一个字组成，简称甘。因境内的六盘山又叫陇山，故又简称陇。元设甘肃行省，明代并入陕西省，清代恢复省治。省会是兰州市。

also known as "Qian" for short. Its capital is Guiyang.

Sichuan Province

The southern area of Jiange in Sichuan Province had been divided into Dongchuan and Xichuan in the early Tang Dynasty, and in Chinese "Chuan" refers to the wide flat plain. Sichuan is the abbreviation of "Chuanxia Silu", which is a collective name of four administrative states (i.e. Yizhou, Zizhou, Lizhou, and Kuizhou) divided by the government of the Song Dynasty. In the Yuan Dynasty, Sichuan was formally established as a province abbreviated as "Chuan". Furthermore, Sichuan Province is also called "Shu" for short, as it was dominated by the State of Shu during the Three Kingdoms Period. Its capital is Chengdu.

Yunnan Province

Yunnan Province takes its name from its location to the south of Yunling Mountains. A legend linked to Yunnan dates back to the Han Dynasty. Somebody told the emperor Han Wudi that clouds appeared over the Bai Cliffs. So he sent a group of men to the south of the empire. When they arrived at the county, the clouds came into existence in the south. So they named the

贵州省

明朝设置贵州省。简称贵。因古代属黔中郡，所以又简称黔。省会是贵阳市。

四川省

唐朝初年在四川省剑阁以南设东川、西川。这里的川，是平川广野的意思。宋代分设益州、梓州、利州等四路，合称"川峡四路"，简称四川，元朝设四川省，简称川。因三国时是蜀国领土，故又简称蜀。省会是成都市。

云南省

因在云岭以南而得名。相传汉武帝时有人在白崖看见彩云，派人追彩云到这里，因为设立的县在彩云的天边，所以叫云南，简称云。因为昆明附近是古代滇国，故又简称滇。清改置云南省。省会是昆明市。

county Yunnan, and "Yun" was the abbreviation. Because Kunming is near the ancient Dian Kingdom, Yunnan is also referred to as Dian. It has been a province since the Qing Dynasty. Its capital is Kunming.

Guangdong Province

Under the Wu Kingdom, Guangdong was given its own name. In the Ming Dynasty, Guangdong Province was established, and "Yue" was the abbreviation as it's located in the Baiyue Region. Its capital is Guangzhou.

Fujian Province

In ancient times there were five cities, Fuzhou, Jianzhou, Quanzhou, Zhangzhou and Tingzhou in the Fujian area. The name Fujian came from the combination of Fuzhou and Jianzhou. In the Ming Dynasty, Fujian Province was established, and "Min" was the abbreviation as it's a residential area of the ancient Chinese Min population. Its capital is Fuzhou.

Hainan Province

Hainan takes its name from Hainan Island, and is abbreviated to "Qiong" because this area had been called

广东省

五代时叫广东。明朝设广东省，因为古是百越（粤）地区，所以简称粤。省会是广州市。

福建省

古代设福州、建州、泉州、漳州、汀州五个州，取前两个州的头一个字就是福建。明朝设福建省，因是古闽族人居住地区，所以简称闽。省会是福州市。

海南省

以海南岛而得名。自秦以后称这一带为琼台、琼州或琼崖，故简称"琼"。1949年为海南特别行政区，1988年改置为海南省。省会是海口市。

Qiongtai, Qiongzhou or Qiongya after the Qin Dynasty. Hainan Special Administrative Region was established in 1949 and changed into Hainan Province in 1988. Its capital is Haikou.

Qinghai Province

Qinghai is named after Qinghai Lake (cyan sea lake), which is briefly named "Qing". Qinghai Province was established in 1928. Its capital is Xining.

Ningxia Hui Autonomous Region

This region is the ancient Xixia district. "Ningxia" means "peaceful Xixia". In 1928, it was detached from Gansu and became a separate province. In 1954, Ningxia was incorporated into Gansu, but was separated from Gansu in 1958 and was reconstituted as an autonomous region for the Hui people. The abbreviation of Ningxia Hui Autonomous Region is "Ning". Its capital is Yinchuan.

Guangxi Zhuang Autonomous Region

Guangxi Province was established in the early years of the Ming dynasty, and became an autonomous region in 1958, namely Guangxi Zhuang Autonomous Region.

青海省

因青海湖而得名。1928年建青海省，简称青。省会是西宁市。

宁夏回族自治区

这里原为古代西夏地区。取夏地安宁的意思，因此叫宁夏。1928年设置宁夏省。1958年改置为宁夏回族自治区，简称宁。自治区的首府是银川市。

广西壮族自治区

明朝初年建广西省，1958年建广西壮族自治区，因古代是桂林郡，故简称桂。自治区的首府是南宁市。

Because this region is the ancient Guilin County, the abbreviation is "Gui". Its capital is Nanning.

Xinjiang Uygur Autonomous Region

This region was the Western Region in ancient times. From the first century BC, the Western Region became a part of the Han Dynasty. As a new territory, it was called Xinjiang (Xin means "new" in Chinese). Xinjiang Province was established in the Qin Dynasty, and became an autonomous region in 1955, with the abbreviation of "Xin". Its capital is Urumqi.

Inner Mongolia Autonomous Region

This region is the Mongolian populated region. In order to distinguish it from Mongolia, it is called "Inner Mongolia". The Inner Mongolia Autonomous Region was established in 1947. Its abbreviation is "Neimenggu", which is the longest abbreviation. Its capital is Hohhot.

新疆维吾尔自治区

古代称西域，公元前 1 世纪起，成为汉王朝的一部分，因为是新开辟的疆土，习惯上称新疆。清光绪年间设置新疆省，于 1955 年改置为新疆维吾尔自治区，简称新。自治区的首府是乌鲁木齐市。

内蒙古自治区

是蒙古族聚居地区，清朝时，为区别外蒙古，习惯上称为内蒙古。1947 年成立内蒙古自治区。简称内蒙古，是所有简称中最长的一个。自治区的首府是呼和浩特。

Chapter 3

Selection from Chinese Classical Literary Works

中国古典文学集锦

China's 5,000-year civilization gave birth to a glorious culture which produced many outstanding masterpieces of classical literary work such as the "Four Great Classical Chinese Novels": *The Water Margin* depicted a peasant uprising; *Journey to the West* represented free spirit; *Romance of the Three Kingdoms* touched mainly on the civil war for control of the country which finally resulted in the establishment of three Chinese Kingdoms; *Red Mansion Dream* dwelt on feudal times family relationships; *Peony Pavilion* praised ideal love. We present here several excellent stamps: *Romance of the Three Kingdoms, The Water Margin, The Peony Pavilion*.

© Zhejiang University Press 2016
Yuehong (Helen) Zhang, *Chinese Cultural Kaleidoscope*,
http://dx.doi.org/10.1631/ZUP.B978-7-308-15903-6_ch3

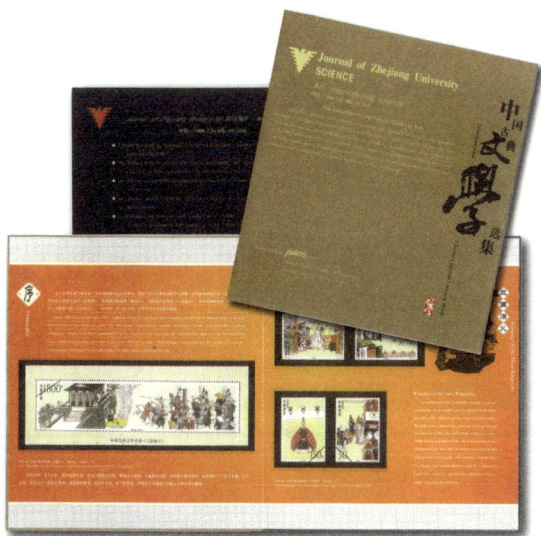

Made in 2005
制于二〇〇五年

　　五千年的华夏文明孕育了中华民族辉煌灿烂的文化，造就了许多名垂史册的文学经典，有描写农民起义的《水浒传》、演绎了封建大家庭生活的《红楼梦》、表现追求自由精神的《西游记》、反映历史演变的《三国演义》、歌颂爱情理想的《牡丹亭》等。在此展示《三国演义》《水浒传》和《牡丹亭》的精美邮票以飨读者。

©浙江大学出版社 2016
张月红，《中国文化万花筒》，
http://dx.doi.org/10.1631/ZUP.B978-7-308-15903-6_ch3

Romance of the Three Kingdoms

Toward the end of the Eastern Han Dynasty China was war-stricken. Rival warlords viciously fought for the throne until three states finally came into being. Cao Cao founded Wei State in northern China, while his rivals Liu Bei and Sun Quan set up Shu State and Wu state respectively in the southwest and southeast of China. The novel touched on the widespread belief that "the world evolves in unification-splitting-reunification cycles". The characteristics of those heroes, such as Zhuge Liang's resourcefulness, Guan Yu's loyalty, and Zhang Fei's intrepidity, are lively representations of the Chinese nation's noble-minded sentiment.

《三国演义》

东汉末年，天下大乱。群雄逐鹿中原，形成三国鼎立之势：曹操占北建魏，刘备据西立蜀，孙权割东南而拥吴。此势暗合了"天下大事，分久必合，合久必分"的历史规律。诸葛亮的智谋、关羽的忠义、张飞的勇猛，栩栩如生地再现了华夏儿女的聪明才智和美好情操。

中国古典文学名著《三国演义》

The Water Margin

During the late Northern Song Dynasty, the heroes of grasslands and swamps, who could no longer bear the cruel oppression of evil officials, fled to the bush and started a very large scale uprising with Liangshan Mountain as its base. Although the uprising was crushed at last, people still took delight in talking about those heroes such as Song Jiang, Wu Song, Lu Zhishen, Lin Chong and Sun Erniang as among the 108 heroes and heroines in Liangshan Mountain.

《水浒传》

　　北宋末年，一群草莽英雄不堪忍受封建统治阶级的压迫，被纷纷逼上梁山，从而掀起了一场规模宏大的农民起义。虽后以失败而告终，然而这些落草为寇的英雄，如宋江、武松、鲁智深、林冲，还有不少女英雄如孙二娘等人，却成为后人津津乐道的"梁山好汉""一百零八将"。

The Peony Pavilion

In the Southern Song Dynasty's early days, there was a young lady named Du Liniang. One bright spring day she strolled in a deserted garden and was inflamed with an aspiration for love. She took a nap near the Peony Pavilion and dreamt a strange dream, in which she met her ideal lover, a romantic scholar who fell in love with her. Later, she fell ill and died of lovesickness after a few months. Three years later, a young man called Liu Mengmei, who looked like the man in her dream, came and dug up Du Liniang's coffin and resuscitated her. Only after many setbacks could they live together forever. The romantic tone permeates the whole story, especially the plot of "Du Liniang's return of the soul because of love". Such an impressive romantic love tragicomedy is on a par with the classical Chinese masterpiece *Red Mansion Dream*.

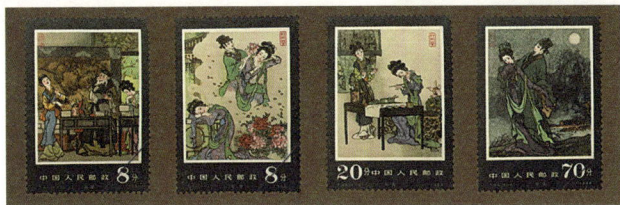

《牡丹亭》

　　南宋初期，官小姐杜丽娘游园伤春，牡丹亭上梦书生，折柳伤情而逝；三年后，书生柳梦梅掘棺助其还魂，共结连理。剧中"杜丽娘慕色还魂"极富浪漫主义气息，其梦幻与现实交织的感人爱情堪与《红楼梦》相媲美。

Chapter 4

Selection from Ancient Chinese Buildings

中国古代建筑集锦

Wonderful Ancient Chinese Buildings

Pagoda of the Six Harmonies

In AD 970, the Lord of Wuyue State gave orders to build the Pagoda of the Six Harmonies, located beside the Qiantang River on the top of Mount Yuelun in Hangzhou, capital of Zhejiang Province, to repress the onrushing tidal water. The name of Six Harmonies has a Buddhist meaning and refers to the six different regulations in Buddhism. The pagoda has thirteen storeys on the outside, but only seven storeys on the inside, forming a pattern of "seven storeys seen and six storeys hidden". Tourists on the balcony of any storey can look at the picturesque landscape of the Qiantang River.

Pagoda of the Six Harmonies before 1899 from a Book Published in 1902
1899年前的六和塔（发现于1902年出版的书籍）

© Zhejiang University Press 2016
Yuehong (Helen) Zhang, *Chinese Cultural Kaleidoscope*,
http://dx.doi.org/10.1631/ZUP.B978-7-308-15903-6_ch4

Made in 2005
制于二〇〇五年

古塔楼阁

六和塔

六和塔位于浙江杭州钱塘江畔月轮山麓，是北宋开宝三年（970），吴越王为镇服汹涌的江潮而建。"六和"指的是佛教的六种规约。六和塔又名六合塔，取"天地四方"之意。塔身外观十三层，内实为七层，呈"七明六暗"的新造型格局，任凭古今游人登塔远眺，钱塘美景尽收眼底。

张月红，《中国文化万花筒》，
http://dx.doi.org/10.1631/ZUP.B978-7-308-15903-6_ch4

Great Wild Goose Pagoda

The Great Wild Goose Pagoda has been used for the safekeeping of Buddhist scriptures and statues brought back by Monk Xuanzang of the Tang Dynasty (AD 652) from ancient India. Of typically traditional Chinese architectural style, it is a five-storey pagoda inside the Temple of Kind Favor to the south of Xi'an City. The name Great Wild Goose Pagoda came from the Buddhist story that ancient Indian monks buried dead wild geese and built a pagoda to commemorate them. Dramatically, it is still standing tall and upright after many years of disturbances.

大雁塔

　　大雁塔是唐代高僧玄奘于唐永徽三年（652），在古城西安慈恩寺内筑五层楼阁式砖塔，用以藏储西天之经典。其雁塔之名取自古印度众僧掩埋坠雁之传说。极具中国传统建筑风格的大雁塔，几经朝代的洗礼，依借佛教经典，奇迹般矗立在华夏中原。

Zhenguo Pagoda

Located in Kaiyuan Temple, Quanzhou City, Zhenguo Pagoda is the tallest pagoda in existence. It was constructed of wood during the Tang Dynasty, and finally rebuilt with bricks in AD 1238, during the Northern Song Dynasty. The height of the tower is 48.24 meters, and on the base and body of the tower are carved diaphanous and lively reliefs. The tower is made of copper and at the top looks like a gourd, which is still standing regally after over seven hundred years.

镇国塔

　　镇国塔是中国现存的最高石塔，位于福建泉州开元寺内。初建于唐咸通年间，原为木塔。几经毁建，于北宋嘉熙二年（1238）改建为楼阁石塔。塔高 48.24 米，塔基、塔身的浮雕生动精致，塔顶用铜铸造成葫芦形塔刹，历时七百余年仍光彩夺目。

Youguo Pagoda

Youguo Pagoda, also called Kaifeng Iron Tower, is a Buddhist pagoda built during the Northern Song Dynasty (AD 1049), and is located in Youguo Temple in the northeast of Kaifeng City. It is the oldest coloured glaze pagoda existing in China. With an octagonal base structure and thirteen storeys, the pagoda is still standing, although the base has been buried underground by the silt of the Yellow River.

佑国寺塔

　　佑国寺塔是宋代（1049）佛塔，位于河南开封市东北隅，佑国寺内。是中国现存最早的琉璃面砖塔。塔为八角形，共十三层。塔基因黄河泛滥淤积已经埋于地面之下，而塔身虽历经磨难，仍屹立不倒。

Yellow Crane Tower

The 51.4-meter-high Yellow Crane Tower (built in AD 223), together with Yueyang Tower in Hunan Province and Tengwang Pavilion in Jiangxi Province, is well known as the Three Famous Towers in southern China. Its name came from the legend that in ancient times, an immortal often passed through, riding on a celestial crane.

Yueyang Tower

Yueyang Tower has been standing to the east of Dongting Lake in Hunan Province since the Tang Dynasty. At the top of the tower you can overlook the Yangtze River on the north side. "The waters of Dongting Lake are the finest and Yueyang Tower is the best under heaven" is known as that famous eulogy on Yueyang Tower written by Fan Zhongyan, a great literatus in the Northern Song Dynasty, who brought Yueyang Tower great fame.

黄鹤楼

耸立于湖北武昌蛇山的黄鹤楼，高 51.4 米，与湖南岳阳楼、江西滕王阁并称"江南三大名楼"，始建于三国时期吴黄武二年（223），相传古时有仙人乘仙鹤屡经此地而得名。黄鹤楼为历代文人荟萃之地。

岳阳楼

岳阳楼最早建于唐朝，矗立于湖南洞庭湖东岸，北望万里长江。自古有"洞庭天下水，岳阳天下楼"之誉。北宋大文学家范仲淹作散文名篇《岳阳楼记》更使其名声大振。

Tengwang Pavilion

Tengwang Pavilion, built in 653 on the Ganjiang River in Nanchang City, gained a good name as the First Pavilion in the West of Southern China. The Tengwang Pavilion Preface by Wang Bo, a notable literatus in the Tang Dynasty, gave the pavilion a niche in the temple of fame.

Penglai Pavilion

Penglai Pavilion, built in 1061 on the Shandong Peninsula on the Bohai Sea has long been known as a wonderful pavilion from which the legend of "Eight Immortals Crossing the Sea" originates.

滕王阁

滕王阁坐落在江西南昌赣江之滨，最早于唐永徽四年（653）建成，素有"西江第一楼"之称。此阁的神韵因唐代文学家王勃所作《滕王阁序》而传名于世。

蓬莱阁

蓬莱阁，始建于北宋嘉祐六年（1061），坐落于山东半岛的蓬莱市，濒临渤海，自古就有"仙境"之称。"八仙过海"的传说即源于此。

Beautiful Ancient Chinese Waterside Towns

Zhouzhuang Town

Located in Suzhou City, Zhouzhuang Town has a long history of more than two thousand years and is well-known for its typical southern Chinese river side scenery featuring small bridges, murmuring streams and elegant dwellings, four lakes enlacing the town, interwinding rivers and old fashioned houses.

Tongli Town

Tongli is a small town with a history of several hundred years and is located beside the Taihu Lake in Suzhou City, Jiangsu Province. With typical Ming and Qing dynasties' architectural style, the town is divided into seven islands by fifteen rivers and encircled by five lakes, with streets, rivers and bridges connecting the town as a whole. The outstanding cultural and historical heritages are "one garden, two halls and three bridges": One garden refers to the famous "Tuisi Garden", two

江南水乡古镇

昆山周庄

周庄已有两千多年的历史。位于江苏苏州市，四湖缠绕，河溪交错，深宅大院，古色古香，一派典型的江南"小桥、流水、人家"。

吴江同里

同里，位于江苏太湖之滨。小镇以明清建筑为主，其五湖怀抱，河流分岛，街沿河而行，桥依水而筑。最出名的建筑风格是"一园、两堂、三桥"：一园是江南名园退思园，两堂是崇本堂、嘉荫堂，三桥是太平桥、吉利桥和长庆桥。

halls refer to "Chongben Hall" and "Jiayin Hall", and three bridges refer to "Taiping Bridge", "Jili Bridge" and "Changqing Bridge".

Wuzhen Town

Wuzhen, located to the north of Tongxiang City, is the hometown of Chinese literatus Mao Dun. The typical landscape of southern China and elegant architecture give birth to a kind of historical and cultural atmosphere for the town, which is known as an "ancient town of thousands of years".

Nanxun Town

Nanxun Town of Huzhou City has many historically famous Chinese structures, such as Jiaye Library, one of the Four Libraries in southern China and Xiaolian Manor, Liu Yong's private manor. In addition, there are the building with a hundred rooms and the old stone bridge built in the Song Dynasty.

桐乡乌镇

乌镇，位于浙江桐乡市北部，是文学巨匠茅盾先生的故乡。典型的江南水乡风情和雅致的居民建筑为其蒙上了一层浓郁的历史和文化气韵。其素有"千年古镇"之美称。

湖州南浔

南浔位于浙江湖州市，名胜古迹有江南四大藏书楼之一的嘉业堂藏书楼、刘镛的庄园小莲庄、百间楼和宋代古石桥等。

Luzhi Town

Luzhi Town, situated in Suzhou City, is well known as the "Land of Bridges" and "Capital of Bridges", since it has lots of water and bridges, which represents the aesthetic craftwork of bridge building in the water country in southern China during the Song Dynasty.

Xitang Town

Xitang Town in Jiashan County is an ancient town with a history going back thousands of years. During the Spring-Autumn and the Warring States periods, it was located on the boundary between the Wu and Yue states.

吴中甪直

甪直，位于江苏苏州市，水多、桥多是其一大特色，汇集了宋代以来苏州水乡集镇桥梁建筑工艺之美，素以"桥梁之乡"闻名于世，且享有江南"桥都"的美称。

嘉善西塘

西塘，位于浙江嘉善县，是一座千年文化古镇。早在春秋战国时期就是吴越两国相交之地，故有"吴根越角"和"越角人家"之称。

Chapter 5

China's Folk Culture

中国民俗文化

The Culture of Chinese Festivals and Holidays

Gently touching on the Chinese festivals cultural context which has grown over several thousand years, deeply inhaling the festivals atmosphere filled with firecrackers and a bumper grain harvest, you will be fully intoxicated by these ancient festival traditions, folk customs, wonderful longings, and cultural heritage.[1]

---

[1] This section is based on a referenced book *Chinese Traditional Festivals* published by Dongfang Press, 2009, in Chinese.

© Zhejiang University Press 2016
Yuehong (Helen) Zhang, *Chinese Cultural Kaleidoscope*,
http://dx.doi.org/10.1631/ZUP.B978-7-308-15903-6_ch5

中国节日（"年"）文化

轻轻地触摸沉淀了上下几千年的中国"年（节日[1]）"文化脉络，深深地吸吮华夏大地上那鞭炮齐鸣、五谷丰登的"年"气味，您会为这神州大地从远古走来的传统节日、风俗民情、美妙憧憬、底蕴文化而痴迷，而陶醉……

Made in 2015
制于二〇一五年

---

[1] 参考于《中国节日——传统文化读本》（严敬群编著，北京：东方出版社，2009）一书及百度百科。

©浙江大学出版社 2016
张月红，《中国文化万花筒》，
http://dx.doi.org/10.1631/ZUP.B978-7-308-15903-6_ch5

Spring Festival (or Chinese New Year)

The Spring Festival, also known as Chinese New Year, has more than 4,000 years of history. It is an important festival celebrated at the turn of the Chinese (lunar) calendar. It falls on the 1st day of the 1st lunar month (usually between late January and early February) each year. It is the most important festival for the Chinese people and it is the time when all family members join together, similar to Christmas which is celebrated in western countries. Before the New Year begins, people completely clean the indoors and outdoors of their homes in order to sweep away any ill-fortune and to make way for good incoming luck. Then people write Spring Festival couplets in black characters on red paper and paste them on their doors and windows, wishing for good fortune, happiness, wealth, longevity and a bright future. The Chinese character "Fu (福)" and red lanterns are also placed on the doors. The whole family will sit together for the annual reunion dinner at Spring Festival Eve and watch the Spring Festival party. The reunion

春节和年

中国民间最隆重欢庆的节日，是农历正月初一的"春节"，又叫"阴历年"，俗称"过年"。据说，"春节"和"年"的概念，最初源于农业，古时人们把谷的生长周期称为"年"，而"过年"的习俗始于殷商，定于西汉，延源至今……

春节是一个欢乐祥和、亲人团聚的日子，离家在外的大人、孩子都要回家过年。农历新年的前一夜，称除夕，又叫团圆夜，全家老小聚在一起熬岁守年，吃年夜饭，尽享天伦之乐。待过年的钟声一响，新的一年就开始了，男女老少盛装打扮，给家族中的长者拜"年"、祝"寿"，给儿童压岁钱，走亲戚，看朋友，相互拜年，祈愿来年好运连连。

dinner is believed to be the most important meal of the year. People will also set off fireworks around midnight to welcome the New Year, called "Shousui".

Traditionally, the Spring Festival in the lunar calendar lasts from December 8th to January 15th; included during this time are Chinese New Year's Eve and the first day of the year as the climax.

Customs: Making New Year's visits, sending New Year's greetings, giving pocket money to children, pasting Spring Festival couplets, eating dumplings.

传统意义上，从农历的腊月初八到正月十五都在"过年"，前后有 30 多天，以除夕和正月初一为"过年"的高潮。

春节的习俗有扫尘、祭祖、贴春联、倒贴"福"字、守岁、放爆竹、拜年、逛庙会、发压岁钱等，喜气洋洋，好不热闹！

Lantern Festival

The Lantern Festival is a Chinese festival celebrated on the 15th day of the first lunar month, during the first night of a full moon. It dates back to the Qin Dynasty. People celebrate it also as the continuation of the Spring Festival. The lanterns are almost always red to symbolize good fortune. During the Lantern Festival, children go out at night to temples, carrying paper lanterns and solve riddles written on the lanterns. People will also make edible lanterns, which are made with sticky rice flour, symbolizing reunion. The main customs include watching lanterns and fireworks, going to the temple fair, guessing lantern riddles.

元宵节

　　春节一去，接着迎来了第二个传统节日——元宵节。据传，元宵节起源于秦朝，至汉文帝时，已下令将一年中第一个月圆之夜、大地回春的夜晚、农历正月十五定为元宵节，意为庆贺新春的延续。人们在这一天赏花灯、猜灯谜、逛庙会、踩高跷、食元宵或汤圆（用糯米粉包成圆形的食品），祈求一年团团圆圆，美美满满。

Tomb-Sweeping Day (or Qingming Festival)

It is one of the 24 seasonal division points in China, falling on April 4–6 each year. Its origin dates back to the Spring-Autumn Period. After the festival, the temperature will rise and rainfall increases. It is not only a seasonal point to guide farm work but also a festival of commemoration. It is the most important day of sacrifice. People offer sacrifices to their ancestors and sweep the tombs of the deceased to show their respect. It is also a time when the sun shines brightly, the trees and soil become green and nature is again renewed. People follow the custom of enjoying spring outings.

Customs: Tomb sweeping, spring outings, kite flying, putting willow branches on gates.

清明节

清明节又叫踏青节，据说始于周朝时期，时间一般在每年公历的 4 月 5 日前后，时值春光明媚、草木吐绿的时节，也正是人们春游（古称踏青）的好时光。

清明是我国二十四节气之一，有"清明时节，点瓜种豆"一说。清明节也是最重要的祭祀节日，是祭祖和扫墓、缅怀逝者的日子。

清明的习俗主要有祭祖扫墓、踏青、植树等。

Dragon Boat Festival (or Duanwu Festival)

The Dragon Boat Festival falls on the 5th day of the 5th month in the lunar calendar, having a history of more than 2,000 years. It was initially for protection from evil and disease. There are several versions of its origin and the most famous one is that it commemorates the death of Qu Yuan (340–278 BC), an upright and honest poet and statesman who is said to have committed suicide by drowning himself in a river.

Two of the most widespread activities for celebration of the Dragon Boat Festival are eating (and preparing) "Zong Zi," which is made of glutinous rice stuffed with different fillings and wrapped in bamboo or reed leaves, and racing dragon boats.

端午节

　　每年农历五月初五，是中华民族古老的传统节日——端午节。其由来多以纪念战国时期因救国无望而于五月初五悲愤投江的伟大爱国诗人屈原之说最为深入人心和历史久远。在民俗文化中，百姓们在这一天，家家吃粽子，水乡竞渡龙舟赛，都与祭奠屈原息息相关。时至今日，有着2000多年历史的端午节，仍是中国各地一个十分盛行的隆重节日。

Mid-Autumn Festival

The Mid-Autumn Festival is celebrated on the 15th day of the 8th month of the lunar calendar, dating back to the Tang Dynasty. It probably began as a harvest festival, and was later given a mythological flavor with legends of Chang'e, the beautiful lady in the moon.

The Mid-Autumn Festival is a time for family members to congregate and enjoy the full moon, an auspicious symbol of reunion. People eat mooncakes and put up sky lights. The round shape of the mooncakes not only symbolizes the moon but also the unity of the family.

The festival celebrates three fundamental concepts which are closely tied to one another: Gathering—such as family and friends coming together, or harvesting crops for the festival; thanksgiving—to give thanks for the harvest or for harmonious unions; praying—asking for conceptual or material satisfaction, such as for babies, a spouse, beauty, longevity or for a good future.

中秋节

　　《唐书·太宗记》就有（农历）"八月十五中秋节"的文字记载。这一天人们对着天上的一轮皓月，观赏祭拜，寄托情怀。中秋节历史悠久，古代帝王有春天祭日、秋天祭月的礼制。后来贵族和文人学士也效仿起来，流传到民间。人们逐渐把中秋赏月与品尝月饼结合在一起，以月之圆兆人之团圆，以饼之圆兆人之常生，用月饼寄托思念故乡、思念亲人之情。

　　中秋的习俗主要有吃月饼、赏月等。

In addition to these Traditional Chinese festivals in existence since ancient times, there are several other holidays in the Gregorian calendar, as follows:

New Year's Day

New Year's Day, January 1st, is the first day of the whole year in the modern Gregorian calendar (or Western calendar), which is the most widely used international standard calendar. In 46 BC, the Roman Emperor Caesar made the day the beginning of the New Year. The New Year's holiday is often marked by fireworks, parades and reflections upon the past year, while looking ahead to the future's possibilities during the New Year. Many people celebrate New Year in the company of loved ones, taking part in traditions meaning to bring luck and success in the coming year. People put on new clothes and say "Happy New Year" to friends.

　　除上述几个中国自古传承的民间节日外，还有：

元　旦

　　新中国成立后把每年公历的 1 月 1 日定为元旦，作为中国的一个节日。也是世界多数国家通称的"新年"，即公历新一年开始的第一天。早在西元前 46 年，古罗马恺撒大帝就把这一天定为西历新年的开始。

International Labour Day

International Labour Day, also known as just Labour Day in some countries, is a celebration of labourers and the working classes that is promoted by the international labour movement, socialists and communists and falls on May 1st each year. It is a world-wide common holiday for working people. While it is truly an international day, its celebration in China is probably one of the largest in the world. This celebration has existed for generations and millions of Chinese people celebrate it. It is often referred to as May Day, due to its position on the calendar. It is also one of the peak periods for travel within the country, and trains and buses are packed with travellers. Unlike many other celebrations in China, May Day is a very simple holiday without any special foods or special costumes or traditional clothing. It is simply a period of rest for workers throughout the country. People use this time to visit relatives, tour historic sites, or simply relax at their homes with their families. It originated with the Chicago City Workers Strike (1886) for the right to work 8 hours a day, also known as the Haymarket Affair.

国际劳动节

　　每年公历 5 月 1 日为国际劳动节，是世界上约有 80 多个国家共度的节日。这源于纪念 1886 年 5 月 1 日，在美国芝加哥城的工人们举行游行示威和罢工斗争，最终赢得一天 8 小时工作时间的权利而定的节日。

International Children's Day

International Children's Day is a festival for the children of the whole world. The Women's International Democratic Federation council meeting was held in Moscow in November 1949. In order to protect the children's right to survival, health and education, and to improve the living environment of children, the meeting decided to set June 1st each year as International Children's Day. Currently, International Children's Day is celebrated in many countries. In China, Children's Day is also celebrated on June 1st. After the People's Republic of China was founded in 1949, the State Council designated a half-day holiday for all primary schools on June 1st. This was later made into a full day's break in 1956 with the announcement by the State Council to make June 1st Children's Day a one-day holiday. Schools usually hold activities such as camping trips or free movies on Children's Day to allow students to have fun. Ceremonies for joining the Young Pioneers of China are usually held on June 1st as well.

国际儿童节

每年公历6月1日为国际儿童节。源于1949年11月，国际民主妇女联合会在莫斯科举行的理事会上为了保障世界各国儿童的生存权、保健权和受教育权，以及为了改善儿童的生活而定的节日。1949年新中国成立后法定每年的6月1日为儿童节，学校放假半天。1956年改为全天。孩子们在这一天会兴高采烈地庆贺自己的节日。

National Day

The National Day falls on October 1st to mark the formation of the People's Republic of China in 1949. Every year there will be different forms of celebration and activities to strengthen people's patriotic consciousness, and strengthen the country's cohesive force.

In 1999, the Chinese Government expanded National Day to allow the people to have an extended holiday from October 1st to 3rd. Traditionally, the festivities begin with the ceremonial raising of the Chinese National flag in Tian'anmen Square in the capital city of Beijing. The flag-raising ceremony is followed first by a large parade exhibiting the country's military forces and then by state dinners and, finally, fireworks displays, which conclude the evening celebrations.

中华人民共和国国庆节

每年的 10 月 1 日为中国的国庆节。这隆重的节日源于 1949 年 10 月 1 日，中华人民共和国在北京天安门广场举行了开国大典。在隆隆的礼炮声中，时任中央人民政府主席毛泽东庄严宣告中华人民共和国成立，并升起第一面五星红旗，广场举行了盛大的阅兵和庆祝游行。新中国的成立实现了中华民族的独立和解放，开创了中国历史的新纪元。1949 年 12 月 3 日，中国政府规定每年的 10 月 1 日为国庆日，并以这一天作为中华人民共和国成立的日子。从此 10 月 1 日就成为中华各族人民隆重欢庆的日子。每年国庆，国家都要举行不同形式的庆祝活动。

1999 年起《全国年节及纪念日放假办法》规定国庆节法定放假日为 3 天，即 10 月 1 日至 3 日。

Blessings Culture

In all cultural phenomena, the blessings and prayers of all peoples all over the world are beneficial and beautiful. Four Chinese characters,福 (Fu) good fortune;禄 (Lu) emolument or prosperity;寿 (Shou) longevity;喜 (Xi) happiness, are four blessings refined over five thousand years of Chinese civilization, and they together compose a set of congratulatory terms to express people's concern with life, hopes for a better life, and the pursuit of their own value in society.

中国"吉祥"文化

在世界文化中，祝福与祈祷是所有民族中都享用的一种美好礼仪。

"福、禄、寿、喜"更是华夏民族五千年文明史上一份来自民间的文化厚礼。每一个字都透着民间百姓对幸福的向往，美好的追求，生命的祈愿，欢喜的祝福。每一句祈愿都是人间吉祥安康的民俗愿景。

Made in 2012
制于二〇一二年

Good fortune—Fu

"Fu", the Chinese character for "good fortune", means longevity, wealth, health, tranquility, and virtue. Sticking and hanging the Chinese character "福 (Fu)" is an important folk custom. In Chinese paintings, the images of bats and Buddha's hands (the Chinese characters for which are homophones, i.e. they share the same pronunciation) convey a "Fu" blessing, implying good luck.

Prosperity or emolument—Lu

"Lu", emolument or wealth, originally meant the official's salary in feudal China. Among folk people, it more often refers to all kinds of wealth, prosperity, fame and social status. People often use deer's homophones to imply good fortune and wealth.

福

福，寓意着安寿富贵康，五福皆吉祥。指人们祈愿万事如意，福星高照。民间的吉祥图案中多以蝙蝠象征"福"气到来。

禄

禄，古指俸禄，寓意高官厚禄。也泛指职位高，待遇优，禄丰厚。民间常以谐音"鹿"指"禄"。

Longevity—Shou

"Shou" means "longevity" that refers to praying for a longer life. The character "Shou" has diverse structures and strokes, giving rise to the circulation of numerous scrolls consisting of a hundred forms of this character. In the reign of the Qing Emperor Kangxi, a huge blue-and-white porcelain vase was created, bearing 10,000 characters for the character "寿 (longevity)" in different forms on its body. People are often blessed with a long life through such patterns as a peach.

Happiness—Xi

"Xi", the Chinese character, originally meant "happiness". People regard anything positive, like a wedding party, childbirth or opening a business as happy events, and form the custom of offering congratulations on these joyful occasions. Double "Xi" (囍) characters are mostly used, especially in wedding ceremonies. The patterns to symbolize happiness are often represented by a magpie.

寿

寿，寓意延年益寿。民俗画中常以"蟠桃"和"仙鹤"祝愿人们长命百岁。

喜

人生如梦，全在一个喜。久旱逢雨、他乡遇故、洞房花烛、金榜题名、升官进爵、财源滚滚、阖家欢乐、延年益寿、天伦之乐，喜不胜收。民间多以喜鹊谐音求喜临门。

Chinese Zodiac

The old Chinese zodiac has been with us for almost two thousand years, and is similar to the 12 constellations in the West, both of which are related to the mysterious astronomical number 12. There are just 12 lunar cycles in a calendar year. The Chinese zodiac is based on a repeating 12-year cycle, an approximation to the 11.86-year cycle of Jupiter. Later, ancient people developed 12 earthly branches to keep track of years. For convenience, personality is mainly determined by the characteristics of animals. The mysterious connection between the 12 animals and people has become a permanent subject. So the 12 animals appear in turn and

Made in 2007

制于二〇〇七年

represent each year, which are: 1. The Rat which is charming (子鼠); 2. The Ox which is patient (丑牛); 3. The Tiger which is sensitive (寅虎); 4. The Rabbit which is articulate (卯兔); 5. The Dragon which is healthy (辰龙); 6. The Snake which is intuitive (巳蛇); 7. The Horse which is popular (午马); 8. The Sheep which is elegant (未羊); 9. The Monkey which is clever (申猴); 10. The Chicken which is a deep thinker (酉鸡); 11. The Dog which is loyal (戌狗); 12. The Pig which is chivalrous (亥猪).

What animal sign were you born under?

I was born in the Year of the Pig, in 2007...

中华民俗——生肖文化

　　中华民俗渊源两千多年的十二生肖（亦称属相）文化，似于西方文化中的十二星座一说，都与十二这个天象数字有着神秘之缘。古人"仰观于天"见一年月圆月缺十二次，故取一年为十二月；测岁星（木星）十二年运一周天，定十二年为一纪。依日之周天运行立十二地支，以纪年法将天干（甲、乙、丙、丁等）地支（子、丑、寅、卯等）巧妙相合。为"天人合一"，而"远取诸物"，选十二种与人类生活密切相关的动物来代之轮回，便是子鼠、丑牛、寅虎、卯兔、辰龙、巳蛇、午马、未羊、申猴、酉鸡、戌狗、亥猪，十二生肖（属相）应运而生。千百年来，生肖（属相）似乎与个人命运息息相随，一层神秘的面纱蒙在了大自然生生衍回的年轮上……

Zi-Year of the Rat—People born in the Year of the Rat are charming, clever and ambitious, having strong talent and interests.

Chou-Year of the Ox—People born in the Year of the Ox are honest and persistent, having clear discretion between love and hate, and succeed in later years.

Yin-Year of the Tiger—People born in the Year of the Tiger are unyielding externally & lenient internally, having an adventurous spirit. They are sensitive.

Mao-Year of the Rabbit—People born in the Year of the Rabbit are gentle, elegant, cheerful and optimistic, having the gift of tongues.

Chen-Year of the Dragon—People born in the Year of the Dragon are healthy and energetic, having strong ideas and long-range planning.

Si-Year of the Snake—People born in the Year of the Snake are deep thinking and mysterious, having the gift of arts.

子鼠年，也称鼠年。生在鼠年的人属鼠，其天性敏锐乐观，兴趣广泛，有极强的适应能力。

丑牛年，也称牛年。生在牛年的人属牛，其天性敦厚踏实，持之以恒，爱憎分明，晚年将宏图大展。

寅虎年，也称虎年。生在虎年的人属虎，其天性外刚内柔，富于冒险。

卯兔年，也称兔年。生在兔年的人属兔，其天性温顺典雅，快活乐观，有语言天赋。

辰龙年，也称龙年。生在龙年的人属龙，其天性精力充沛，气宇轩昂，有远大目标。

巳蛇年，也称蛇年。生在蛇年的人属蛇，其天性深思熟虑，神秘莫测，有艺术天才。

*Wu-*Year of the Horse—People born in the Year of the Horse are open and romantic, free and frank, having heroic spirits.

*Wei-*Year of the Sheep—People born in the Year of the Sheep are humane, exquisite and circumspect, having initiative.

*Shen-*Year of the Monkey—People born in the Year of the Monkey are lively, clever, lenient and confident, good at competition.

*You-*Year of the Chicken—People born in the Year of the Chicken are very fashionable, vigorous and social, good at pondering.

*Xu-*Year of the Dog—People born in the Year of the Dog are loyal, humble, upright and brave, having a strong sense of obligation.

*Hai-*Year of the Pig—People born in the Year of the Pig are very kind, frank and generous, having good relations with others.

午马年，也称马年。生在马年的人属马，其天性开朗大方，自由奔放，有英雄气概。

未羊年，也称羊年。生在羊年的人属羊，其天性温厚儒雅，细腻周到，有进取心。

申猴年，也称猴年。生在猴年的人属猴，其天性活泼机灵，宽厚自信，求知欲望强。

酉鸡年，也称鸡年。生在鸡年的人属鸡，其一生追求时尚，神采奕奕，广交朋友，善于思考。

戌狗年，也称狗年。生在狗年的人属狗，其天性忠诚本分，纯朴谦虚，勇敢义气。

亥猪年，也称猪年。生在猪年的人属猪，其性情率直，心地善良，慵懒大方，人缘好。

Chapter 6

The Chinese Style of Writing
中华文苑

four Treasures of Study in China

Writing brush, inkstick, paper, and inkstone are called "Four Treasures of Study" in China. Unique features of these four have helped the achievement of elegant styles of Chinese calligraphy and painting. During the past 2,000 years, the four treasures have developed with their rich cultural heritage and produced more and more charm. The "Hu Brush", made in Huzhou, Zhejiang, was given the name in the Yuan dynasty (AD 1271–1368); the "Hui Inkstick", produced in ancient Huizhou (now southern Anhui) can be traced back to the Song dynasty (AD 960–1279); "Xuan Paper" was named for its production place, Xuanzhou (now Jingxian, Anhui), in the Tang dynasty (AD 618–907); and "Duan Inkstone" was also named after its original place, Duanxi (now Zhaoqing, Guangzhou) in the Tang Dynasty.

© Zhejiang University Press 2016

Yuehong (Helen) Zhang, *Chinese Cultural Kaleidoscope*,

http://dx.doi.org/10.1631/ZUP.B978-7-308-15903-6_ch6

文房四宝——笔、墨、纸、砚

中华民族灿烂文化中的笔、墨、纸、砚堪称"文房四宝"。这四种文具的独特性能，催生了汉文字的书法艺术，造就了中国画的笔墨风格。两千年来，具有深厚文化底蕴的湖笔（始于元朝）、徽墨（始于宋朝）、宣纸（始于唐朝）、端砚（始于唐朝）在中国历史的渊源长河中挥洒传承着中华民族的文化魅力。

Made in 2006
制于二〇〇六年

©浙江大学出版社 2016
张月红，《中国文化万花筒》，
http://dx.doi.org/10.1631/ZUP.B978-7-308-15903-6_ch6

Chinese Calligraphy

The "hieroglyphic (⊛)" of Chinese characters originated as far back as 6,000 years ago, in the area of the middle reaches of the Yellow River, during the "Yang Shao Culture" period. Chinese calligraphy has long represented and followed the unique and charming beauty of oriental art, tracking the history of art closely, from the dynasties of Xia, Shang, and Zhou (c 2070–770 BC), through the period of the Warring States of 770–221 BC when inscriptions on bones, tortoise shells, or bronze appeared, to the Qin Dynasty, when Zhuan-Shu (龍, simplified hieroglyphic) and Li-Shu (龍, similar to silkworm head & swallowtail) were created, to the dynasties of Eastern Han, Three Kingdoms, and Jin, when Kai-Shu (龍, straight in line, square in shape), Xing-Shu calligraphies (龍, writing on the run) and Cao-Shu (龍, one-stroke writing) were shaped.

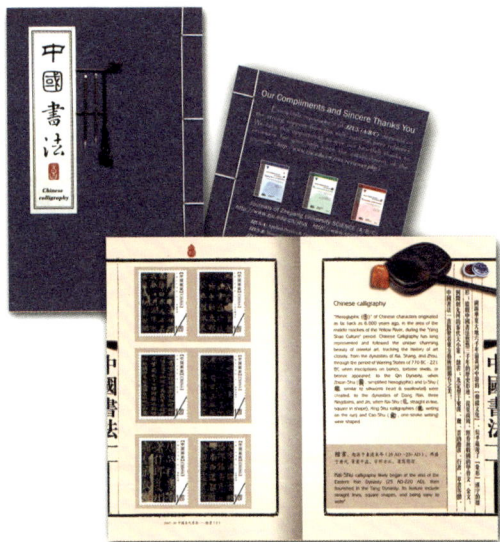

Made in 2011
制于二〇一一年

中国书法——篆、隶、楷、行、草

溯源华夏大地约6000年前黄河中游的"仰韶文化"，似乎萌发了"象形"汉字的雏形；纵观中国书法悠悠三千年的历史形迹（以安阳殷墟甲骨文发现为证而前伸），从夏商周，经春秋战国的甲骨文、金文，到开创先河的秦代大小篆、隶书，及定型于东汉、魏、晋的楷书、行书、草书等体，中国书法一直散发着东方艺术的独有之美！

Kai-Shu, calligraphy most likely began at the end of the Eastern Han Dynasty (AD 25–220), and then flourished in the Tang Dynasty. Its features include straight lines, square shapes, and being easy to write.

Zhuan-Shu and Li-Shu, or "Official Script" first came into being about 400 years before the Qin Dynasty (221–207 BC), and was established officially in the Han Dynasty (202 BC–AD 220). It features with its preservation of ancient pictographs.

楷书，起源于东汉末年（25—220），兴盛于唐代。笔画平直，字形方正，书写简洁。

篆书和隶书，始于秦皇朝前约400年，定型于汉代，尚保存着古代象形文字的明显特点。汉字是由篆书发展为隶书，又由隶书发展为真书，是中国字形体变迁史中的一个重要转折点，隶书以前多以象形兼表意。

The "four Gentlemen" in Painting

Plum in winter, orchid in spring, bamboo in summer and chrysanthemum in autumn, together they bloom in all seasons and are referred to as the "four gentlemen" in Traditional Chinese painting culture. The four plants are metaphoric symbols expressing sublime nobility, elegance, tenacity, and purity, respectively.

The plum blooms in winter, showing its nobility and unyielding character.

中国书画四君子——梅、兰、竹、菊

梅（冬）、兰（春）、竹（夏）、菊（秋），各尽春夏秋冬。常在国画里被尊为"花草四君子"。各自表征着华夏文化里的高雅、清逸、正直与淡泊的四种品格。历代文人墨客多以梅兰竹菊抒情画意，表达高雅气节。

Made in 2013
制于二〇一三年

Plum. A poem below, written by Wang Anshi (AD 1021 –1086), a political poet in the Song Dynasty

Plum Blossom

At a wall corner some plum trees grow,

Alone against cold, white blossoms blow.

Aloof one knows they aren't the snow,

As faint through air soft fragrances flow.[1]

Orchid. An orchid blooms in spring with peace and purity. A beautiful poem, written by Tao Yuanming (AD 376–427) in the Eastern Jin Dynasty.

Orchids in Breezes

In blossom orchids grow in charm and grace,

Awaiting clear breezes in the courtyard.

With fresh aroma rippling in embrace,

Making them different from wild weeds.

---

[1] The four poems translation information is primarily from XDF.CN; EN8848.com. cn and then http etc.

梅，独开腊月，傲霜立雪。北宋政治诗人王安石（1021—1086）有一首《梅花》诗：

"墙角数枝梅，凌寒独自开。遥知不是雪，为有暗香来。"道尽梅花的幽香高雅。

兰，春兰幽香，与世无争。东晋田园诗人陶渊明（376—427）有一首《幽兰》诗：

"幽兰生前庭，含薰待清风。清风脱然至，见别萧艾中。"说尽兰花的清逸洁净。

Bamboo. Bamboo is tall and straight, with a strong central stem marked with nodes, and represents tenacity and integrity.

Here is a poem written by Zheng Banqiao (AD 1693–1765), a famous painter in the Qing Dynasty.

Bamboo and Rock

Between broken rocks striking my root deep,
I bite the mountain green and won't let go.
From whichever direction the winds leap,
I remain strong, though dealt many a blow.

Chrysanthemum. Chrysanthemum blooms defiantly against the frost after a multitude of other flowers have withered, and represents purity and tenacity.

A poem below, written by Yuan Zhen (AD 779–831) in the Tang Dynasty.

Chrysanthemum

Surrounded by fall petals like ribbon, taking after Tao's home,
Wrapping the fences all over, sunset over the cottage dome.
It's not that I have special preference for the chrysanthemum,
After these blooms in the fall, there's nothing left to blossom.

竹，刚而挺拔，竹节清气。清代书画家郑板桥（1693—1765）有一首《竹石》诗：

"咬定青山不放松，立根原在破岩中。千磨万击还坚劲，任尔东西南北风。"画出了竹子的质本气节。

菊，怒放于凋零之秋，享有菊贵之尊。

唐朝诗人元稹（779—831）有一首《菊花》诗：

"秋丛绕舍似陶家，遍绕篱边日渐斜。不是花中偏爱菊，此花开尽更无花。"绘出了秋菊的清雅淡泊。

Chapter 7

Chinese Philosophy
中国哲学

Six Ancient Chinese Thinkers of the Pre-Qin Period[1]

The place which philosophy occupies in Chinese civilization is comparable to that of religion in some other civilizations. In China, philosophy has been every educated person's concern. According to the tradition of Chinese philosophy, its function is not the increase in positive knowledge, but the elevation of the mind, a reaching out for what is beyond the present actual world, for obtaining values that are higher than the moral ones. In the olden days, if a man was not educated at all, the first education he received was in philosophy. For example, the Four Books, (the *Confucian Analects,* the *Book of Mencius,* the *Great Learning, and* the *Doctrine of the Mean*), which represent the most important texts of Confucianist philosophy, have been the Bible of the Chinese people.

---

[1] Referenced from Fung Yulan's *A Short History of Chinese Philosophy.*

© Zhejiang University Press 2016

Yuehong (Helen) Zhang, *Chinese Cultural Kaleidoscope,*
http://dx.doi.org/10.1631/ZUP.B978-7-308-15903-6_ch7

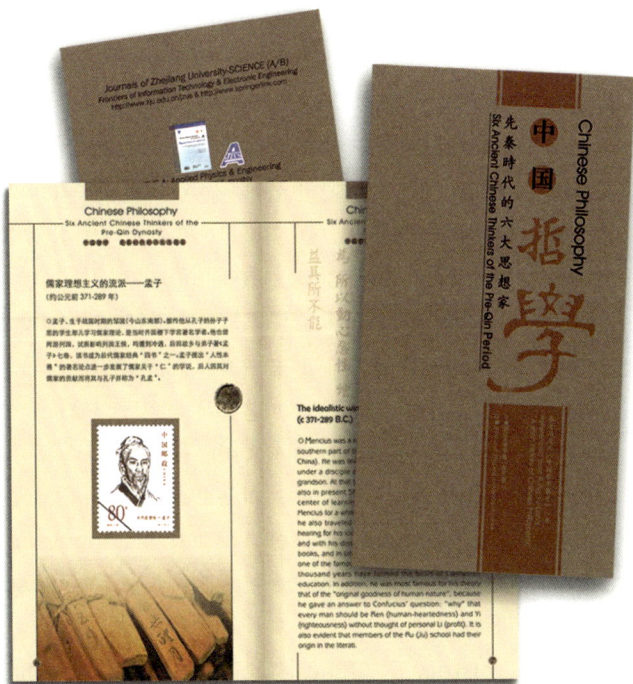

Made in 2014

制于二〇一四年

Chinese philosophy has existed for about 3,000 years, starting with Xia, Shang and Zhou around 2000–722 BC, passing through the Pre-Qin Period, from the Spring-Autumn Period (722–480 BC) to the Warring States Period (479–220 BC), the Qin (221–206 BC) and Han (202 BC–AD 220) dynasties. Then it was followed by metaphysics during the Wei (AD 220–266) and Jin (AD 265–420) dynasties, the Buddhist philosophy during the Sui (AD 581–618) and Tang (AD 618–907) dynasties, Neo-Confucianism in the Song (AD 960–1279) and Ming (AD 1368–1644) dynasties, practical philosophy in the Ming and Qing dynasties (AD 1506–1840), modern new learning (AD 1840–1911), and then the present modern philosophy (from AD 1919). In the history of Chinese philosophy, the Pre-Qin Period (551–221 BC) cannot only be seen as a germinal source for many schools of traditional Chinese philosophy, but also as the first brilliant era.

In the history of Chinese philosophy, during the period from the fifth to the third centuries BC, the number of schools of thought was so great that the Chinese referred to them as the "Hundred Schools", among which

先秦时代的六大思想家[1]

哲学在中国传统文化中的地位历来可与宗教在其他文化中的地位相比拟。哲学在古代中国，是知识教育最重要的内容之一。中国哲学的精髓不在于增长知识，而在于提升人的心灵，超越现实的领悟，高于道德的价值。旧时，儒家哲学思想的代表作——《论语》《孟子》《大学》和《中庸》，常被作为读书人必学的精神启蒙之书。换言之，"四书"在中国人心中的地位类似于西方人心中的《圣经》。

中国哲学在3000多年漫长的历史中，萌芽于夏、商、周三代，先后经历了先秦诸子学时期（秦以前的春秋：前722—前480；战国：前479—前220）、秦汉哲学时期（秦：前221—前206，汉：前202—220）、魏晋玄学时期（魏：220—266与晋：265—420）、隋唐佛学时期（隋：581—618；唐：618—907）、宋明理学时期（两宋：960—1279；至明代：1368—1644）、明清实学时期（明

---

[1] 这一部分内容参考了《英汉中国哲学简史》，冯友兰著，赵复三译，南京：江苏文艺出版社，2012。

© 浙江大学出版社 2016

张月红，《中国文化万花筒》，

http://dx.doi.org/10.1631/ZUP.B978-7-308-15903-6_ch7

Confucianism, Taoism and Mohism were the three main streams of Chinese thought. Here the word "School" is a translation of the Chinese character "Jia" (Chia) which means that there were persons (or teachers) who taught their own ideas in a private capacity, for example, Ru Jia (Ju Chia) or the School of Literati known in Western literature as the Confucian School. Actually, in these schools there were scholars as well as thinkers, who were the teachers of the ancient classics and thus the inheritors of the ancient cultural legacy. Confucius, to be sure, is the leading figure of this school and may rightly be considered as its founder. Here we introduce six important ancient Chinese thinkers from these schools during the Pre-Qin Period. They are Confucius, Mencius, Xun Zi (Hsün Tzu), Lao Zi (Tzu), Zhuang Zi (Tzu), and Mo Zi (Tzu), respectively.

朝正德年间至清代鸦片战争前夕：1506—1840）、近代新学时期（晚清至民国时期：1840—1911）和现当代哲学时期（1919—　）等发展阶段。而先秦诸子学一直被视为中国传统哲学众多流派的生发源头，也被尊为中国哲学史上第一个灿烂的时代。

　　中国哲学以华夏民族的认识为起源，至春秋末期、战国时代出现了百家争鸣的局面。众所周知，儒家、道家与墨家是先秦诸子中代表中国古代哲学思想的最重要的几个流派。特别是儒家学派，儒的本意是读书人（文士）或学者。在西方被称为"孔子学派"，主要由学者和思想家所组成。他们讲授古代的经书，也是古代文化的传承者。孔子无疑是这一学派的领袖人物，也是这一学派的创始人。这里主要介绍先秦诸子学派中最有代表性的六位古代思想家，他们分别是儒家学派的孔子、孟子和荀子，道家的老子和庄子，以及墨家的墨子。

Sage of Chinese culture—Confucius (551–479 BC)

The three greatest figures of the School of Literati in the Pre-Qin Period were Confucius (551–479 BC), Mencius (c 371–289 BC), and Xun Zi (Hsün Tzu) (c 298–238 BC).

Confucius's family name was Kong (K'ung), and his personal name was Qiu (Chiu). He was born in the State of Lu, in the southern part of the present-day Shandong Province in East China. His ancestors had been members of the ducal house in the Shang Dynasty. Because of political troubles, his family, before the birth of Confucius, had lost its noble position and migrated to Lu. He was poor in his youth, but entered the government of Lu and by the time he was fifty had reached a high official rank. As a result of political intrigue, however, he was soon forced to resign his post and go into exile. For the next thirteen years he travelled from one state to another, always hoping to find an opportunity to realize his ideal of political and

中国文化的先哲
——孔子（前551—前479）

先秦儒家学派中三个最重要的人物是孔子、孟子和荀子。

孔子，姓孔，名丘，字仲尼，生于春秋末期的鲁国（今山东省南部）。祖先为周朝之前的商朝贵族，到孔子出生前已经破落，迁居鲁国。孔子50岁前曾在鲁国官至高位，后因政治诬陷迫于辞官，继而周游列国，教书育人十三载，传说追随其学生达三千多，其多位弟子也成为时代俊杰而留名史册。后由弟子整理编撰的《论语》已成世代研究孔子思想的典籍，这一切奠定了孔子作为中国历史

social reform. Nowhere, however, did he succeed, and finally as an old man he returned to Lu, where he died three years later in 479 BC.

Confucius was the first private teacher in Chinese history. Thus he had several thousand students, of whom several became famous thinkers and scholars. His ideas are the best known through the *Lun Yu* or *Confucian Analects*, a collection of his and his students' scattered sayings, which were compiled by some of his disciples.

Confucius was the founder of the Ru (Ju) School known in the West as the Confucian School, which concentrated on the study of the Liu Yi, or Six Classics: They are the *Shi or Book of Odes*, the *Shu* or *Book of History*, the *Li* or *Rites*, the *Yue* or *Music*, the *Yi* or *Book of Changes*, and the *Chun Qiu* or *Spring and Autumn Annuals*, and emphasized matters concerning human-heartedness and righteousness. Because his followers of this school were at the same time scholars and specialists in the Six Classics, the school became known as the School of Literati. Or, in other words, "members of the Ru (Ju) School had their origin in the literati".

上第一位教育家的地位。同时被尊为儒家学派创始人的孔子崇尚"礼治"和"仁政"，提倡"忠恕"和"中庸"，其晚年亲自修订的六经（《诗》《书》《礼》《乐》《易》和《春秋》）及与后人编纂的四书（《论语》《孟子》《大学》和《中庸》）一道作为儒家经典而被后人学习研究，而儒家学派也多以学者派著称。

孔子的"吾十有五而志于学，三十而立，四十而不惑，五十而知天命，六十而耳顺，七十而从心所欲，不逾矩"真实地写照了他好学而智慧的一生。

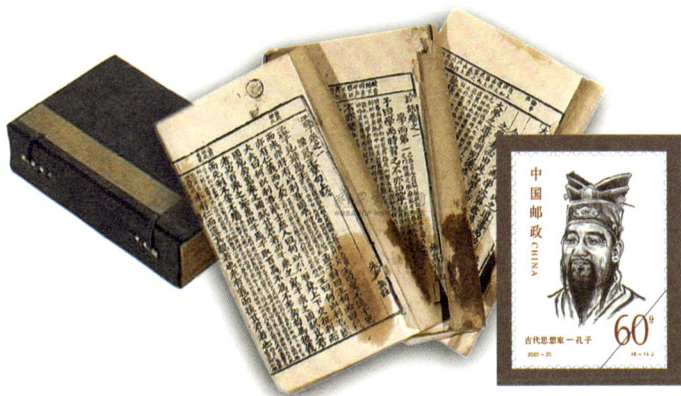

Related to Confucius's spiritual realm, we can quote what he said: "At fifteen I set my heart on learning. At thirty I could be steadfast. At forty I have no doubts. At fifty I knew the Decree of Heaven. At sixty I was already obedient to this Decree. At seventy I could follow the desires of my mind without overstepping the boundaries of what is right" (*Analects*, II, 4).

The idealistic wing of Confucianism— Mencius (c 371–289 BC)

Mencius was a native of the State of Zou (Tsou), in the southern part of the present-day Shandong province in East China. He was linked with Confucius through his studies under a disciple of Zi-Si (Tzu-ssu), who was Confucius's grandson. At that time, the Kings of Qi (Ch'i), a larger state, also in present-day Shandong, supported and established a center of learning which they called Jixia (Chi-hsia). Mencius for a while was one of these eminent scholars, but he also travelled to other states, vainly trying to get a hearing for his ideas among their rulers. Finally, he retired and with his disciples composed

儒家理想主义流派代表
——孟子（约前371—前289）

孟子，生于战国时期的邹国（今山东南部）。据传他从孔子的孙子子思的学生那儿学习儒家理论，是当时齐国稷下学宫著名学者。他也曾周游列国，试图影响列国王侯，均遭到冷遇。后回故乡与弟了著《孟子》七卷，该书成为后代儒家经典"四书"之一。孟子提出的"人性本善"的著名论点进一步发展了儒家关于"仁"的学说，后人因其对儒家的贡献而将其与孔子并称为"孔孟"。

the *Mencius* in seven books, and in later times it was honored by being made one of the famous "Four Books", which for the past one thousand years have formed the basis of Confucian education. In addition, he was most famous for his theory of the "original goodness of human nature", and he thus gave an answer to Confucius's question as to why every man should have Ren (human-heartedness) and Yi (righteousness) without thought of personal Li (profit). It is also evident that members of the Ru (Ju) School had their origin in the literati.

The realistic wing of Confucianism— Xun Zi (c 298–238 BC)

Xun Zi's personal name was Kuang. He was a native of the State of Zhao (Chao) in the southern part of the present-day Hebei and Shanxi provinces in China. When he was fifty he went to the State of Qi (Ch'i), where he was probably the last great thinker of the academy of Ji-Xia (Chi-hsia), the great centre of learning at that time. Among the literati, Xun is best known because of his theory that human nature is originally evil. This

儒家现实主义流派代表
——荀子（约前298—前238）

荀子，名况，字卿，赵国（今河北、山西南部）人。
与孟子相同，荀子五十岁到齐国的稷下学宫，大概是稷下
的最后一位大思想家。《荀子》一书为其著作集。其思想与
孟子有很大不同，主张"人性本恶"须加以教养，认为价
值来自文化，而文化皆为人所创造，其理论可称为文化哲
学。他突出人的价值，认为在宇宙中，人与天地同等重要。

is directly opposed to Mencius, according to whom human nature is originally good. So Xun's thought is the antithesis of that of Mencius. Actually, Xun's philosophy may be called a philosophy of culture. His general thesis is that everything that is good and valuable is the product of human effort. Value comes from culture and culture is the achievement of man. It is by this philosophy that man has the same importance in the universe as Heaven and Earth.

The main founder of Taoism—Lao Zi (c 571–471 BC)

His family name was Li and his personal name Er. According to tradition, Lao Zi was a native of the State of Chu, in the southern part of the present-day Henan Province in China. Although his exact dates are uncertain, the book bearing his name, the *Lao Zi* (Tzu), and in later times also known as the *Dao De Jing* (*Tao Te Ching*, or *Classic of the Way and Power*), has therefore been traditionally regarded as the first philosophical work in Chinese history. Among the laws that govern the changes

道家的创始人之一
——老子（约前571—前471）

老子，姓李，名耳，字聃，历来以老子为楚国（今河南省南部）人。其代表作品《老子》（又名《道德经》）一书被认为是中国第一部哲学著作。人们常说的"物极必反"即源自老子的"反者道之动"思想，其含有朴素的辩证法观点。若谈及处世为人，老子道："知常曰明。"而论及为政纲领，老子智道："我无为，而民自化；我好静，而民自正；我无事，而民自富；我无欲，而民自朴。"老子被道家学派尊为创始人之一。

道家与儒家学派在某些政治纲领上有相同点，如他们认为在理想国里，国家首脑应当是一个圣人。而不同之处在于：儒家认为，圣人治国，应为大众多做事情；而道家认为，圣人治国，不要忙于做事，而是要废除过去本不应做的事情，强调"无为而治"。

in things, the most fundamental is that "when a thing reaches one extreme, it reverts from it", the idea for which no doubt comes from Lao Zi. "Reversing is the movement of the Dao (Tao)." On human conduct, Lao Zi warns us: "Not to know the invariable and to act blindly is to go to disaster"and "practice enlightenment". It is a well-known fact that Lao was the main founder of the Taoist School, and Taoism emphasizes what is natural and spontaneous in people. Although there are many comparisons between the similarities and differences of the two schools of political theory, here Taoists agree with the Confucianists that the ideal state is one which has a sage as its head who can and should rule. The difference is that according to Confucianists, when a sage becomes the ruler, he should do many things for the people, whereas according to the Taoists, the duty of the sage ruler is not to do things, but rather to undo or not to do at all. For this reason, as Lao Zi said in the *Lao Zi:* "The more restrictions and prohibitions there are in the world, the poorer the people will be. The more sharp weapons the people have, the more troubled the country

道家最有影响的人物
——庄子（约前369—前286）

庄子，名周，字子休，蒙国（今山东、河南两省边境）人，大概是早期道家中最伟大的思想家之一。毕生过着隐士式的生活，但其思想和著述已驰名当时。他也主张"无为而治"，但所持理由与老子不完全相同，更为强调天与人的不同，主张摒弃人文虚伪，顺从天道自然。据传为其代表作的《庄子》是一部早期道家思想的汇编，内含有庄子的诸多作品，其作品想象丰富，妙趣横生，善于以寓言说理，是先秦散文的典范。庄子最早提出"内圣外王"的思想，对后世儒家有着深远的影响。

will be. The more cunning craftsmen there are, the more pernicious contrivances will appear. The more laws that are promulgated, the more thieves and bandits there will be."

The greatest person of the early Taoists—Zhuang Zi (c 369-286 BC)

His personal name was Zhou (Chou), a native of the little State of Meng, on the border between the present-day Shandong and Henan provinces. He is perhaps the greatest of the early Taoists. Similar to the descriptions in the Chinese philosophy books, "members of the Taoism School had their origin in the hermits". He lived a hermit's life but was nevertheless famous for his ideas and writings. Zhuang Zi advocated government through non-government, but for somewhat different reasons, compared to those of Lao Zi. He emphasized the distinction between what is of nature and what is of man. The book entitled the *Zhuang Zi* (*Chuang-tzu*), is a collection of various Taoist writings, and in the first chapter which is entitled "The Happy Excursion", there is

孔子的第一个反对者
——墨子（约前479—前381）

墨子，名翟，其生卒年代及出生地尚不详，可能出生于楚国或宋国（现河南东部、山东西部）。墨子以及他创立的以侠士为主体的墨家学派，在先秦其声誉及影响力与孔子的儒家学派不相上下，当时并称为"显学"。墨子抨击儒家的主张华而不实。与儒家的"天命""爱有差等"等观点相对立，他提出了"兼爱""非攻""非命"等主张。比较两人南辕北辙的不同主张十分有趣。简言之，孔子对古代文明的态度是理性合理化，而墨子持批判态度；孔子是一位文雅有修养的君子，墨子更像是一位充满战斗精神的布道家。他说教的宗旨是反对传统的典章制度，反对孔子和儒家的诸多理论。代表作品《墨子》是墨翟及其后学的著作汇编，其中包含有不少朴素的唯物主义思想。

a simple text, full of amusing stories. Their underlying idea is that there are varying degrees in the achievement of happiness. A free development of our natures may lead us to a relative kind of happiness, and absolute happiness is achieved through a higher understanding of the nature of things.

The first opponent of Confucius—Mo Zi (c 479–381 BC)

The next major philosopher after Confucius was Mo Zi (Tzu). His family name was Mo and his personal name was Di (Ti). Although his exact dates and life are uncertain, he probably lived sometime within the years 497–381 BC, and he might have been a native of Song (Sung), in the present-day Henan and Shandong provinces. The main source for the study of his thoughts is the book bearing his name, the *Mo Zi* (*Tzu*), which is a collection of writings by his followers as well as by himself. Mo Zi was the founder of a school known after his name as the Mohist School, in which members had their origin in the knights. In ancient times his fame was as great as that of Confucius. The contrast between Confucius and Mo Zi is interesting. In short, Confucius was the rationalizer and justifier of the ancient civilization, while Mo Zi was its critic. Confucius was a refined gentleman, while Mo Zi was a militant preacher. A major aim of his preaching was to oppose both the traditional institutions and practices, and the theories of Confucius and the Confucianists.

Chapter 8

A Sight of Modern China—Beijing 2008 Olympic Games

现代中国一景
——2008北京奥运

Made in 2008
制于二〇〇八年

Beijing 2008 Olympic Games—China's Strengths

You cannot imagine how spectacular the 2008 Beijing Olympics were. In total, 10,942 athletes from 204 National Olympic Committees came to Beijing for a common goal, to enjoy the Olympic spirit. During the 2008 Beijing Olympic Games, Chinese athletes made remarkable achievements, winning 51 gold medals, ranking first in the world; the US won 36 gold medals, ranking second (see Fig. 2). The total medals won by China (gold, silver, copper) were 100, ranking second while the US was first with 110 total medals. As of today, this represents the best result achieved by the China Sport Olympic Teams.

© Zhejiang University Press 2016

Yuehong (Helen) Zhang, *Chinese Cultural Kaleidoscope*,

http://dx.doi.org/10.1631/ZUP.B978-7-308-15903-6_ch8

2008北京奥运会——中国奖牌亮点

2008 年的北京奥运会盛况空前，来自 204 个国家和地区的 10942 名运动员参加了本届奥运会。中国运动员在本届奥运会取得了骄人的成绩（见图 2），金牌得奖数排名世界第一（51 枚），美国第二（36 枚）。中国所获总奖牌（金、银、铜）合计为 100 枚，排名第二，美国第一（110 枚）。这也是中国体育奥运榜上最好的成绩。

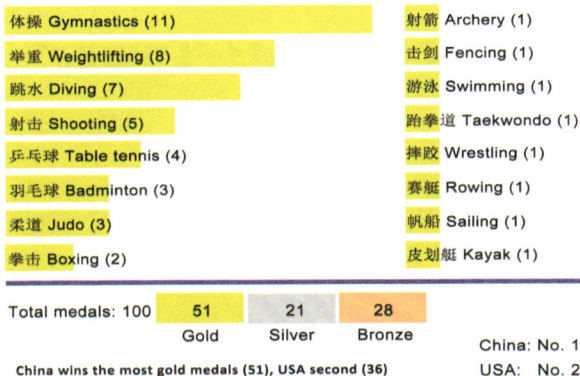

体操 Gymnastics (11)
举重 Weightlifting (8)
跳水 Diving (7)
射击 Shooting (5)
乒乓球 Table tennis (4)
羽毛球 Badminton (3)
柔道 Judo (3)
拳击 Boxing (2)

射箭 Archery (1)
击剑 Fencing (1)
游泳 Swimming (1)
跆拳道 Taekwondo (1)
摔跤 Wrestling (1)
赛艇 Rowing (1)
帆船 Sailing (1)
皮划艇 Kayak (1)

Total medals: 100 | 51 Gold | 21 Silver | 28 Bronze

China: No. 1
USA: No. 2

China wins the most gold medals (51), USA second (36)

Fig 2　China's Olympic Record in the Beijing 2008 Olympic Games
图2　2008年北京奥运会中国金牌榜

©浙江大学出版社 2016
张月红，《中国文化万花筒》，
http://dx.doi.org/10.1631/ZUP.B978-7-308-15903-6_ch8

北 Beibei   京 Jingjing   欢 Huanhuan

迎 Yingying   你 Nini

Official Mascots—Fuwas' Story[1]

Here is an interesting story for you to read that describes the Olympic mascots.

The official mascots of the Beijing 2008 Olympic Games, combining five Fuwas' names together express

----

[1] The brief introduction about Fuwa mascots is based on a reference by Xinhua News Agency November 11, 2005 (http://en.beijing2008.com).

"Bei Jing Huan Ying Ni (北京欢迎你)!", in English "Welcome to Beijing!" The designer, Han Meilin, a famous Chinese artist, was desirous that like the five colours of the Olympic rings, the Fuwas would carry the message of friendship and peace, and blessings from China, to children all over the world. Designed to express the playful qualities of five little children who form an intimate circle of friends, the Fuwas also embody the natural characteristics of four of China's most popular animals—the Fish, the Panda, the Tibetan Antelope, the Swallow—plus the Olympic Flame.

Each Fuwa has a rhyming two-syllable name— a traditional way of expressing affection for children in China. Beibei (贝贝) is the Fish, Jingjing (晶晶) is the Panda, Huanhuan (欢欢) is the Olympic Flame, Yingying (迎迎) is the Tibetan Antelope and Nini (妮妮) is the Swallow. In their origins and their headpieces, you can see the five elements of nature—the sea, forest, fire, earth and sky—all stylistically rendered in ways that represent

the deep traditional influences of Chinese folk art and ornamentation. Each Fuwa symbolizes a different blessing and will honor this tradition by carrying the blessings to the children of the world. Prosperity, happiness, passion, health and good luck were spread to every continent as the Fuwas carried their invitation to Beijing 2008 to every part of the globe.

In China's traditional culture and art, the fish and water designs are symbols of prosperity and the harvest. So Beibei carries the blessing of prosperity. A fish is also a symbol of surplus in Chinese culture, another measure of a good year and a good life. The ornamental lines of the water-wave designs are taken from well-known Chinese paintings of the past. Among the Fuwas, Beibei is known to be gentle and pure. Strong in water sports, she reflects the blue Olympic ring.

Jingjing makes children smile. You can see his joy in the charming naivety of his dancing pose and the lovely wave of his black and white fur. As a national treasure and a protected species, pandas are adored by people everywhere. The lotus designs in Jingjing's head-dress, which are inspired by the porcelain paintings of the Song Dynasty (AD 960–1234), symbolize the lush forest

and the harmonious relationship between man and nature. Jingjing was chosen to represent our desire to protect nature's gifts, and to preserve the beauty of nature for all generations. Jingjing is charmingly naïve and optimistic. He is an athlete noted for strength, who represents the black Olympic ring.

Huanhuan is a child of fire, symbolizing the Olympic flame and the passion of sport—and passion is the blessing he bestows. Huanhuan stands in the centre of

the Fuwas as the core embodiment of the Olympic spirit. And while he inspires all with the passion to run faster, jump higher and be stronger, he is also open and inviting. Wherever the light of Huanhuan shines, the

inviting warmth of Beijing 2008, and the wishful blessings of the Chinese people, can be felt. The fiery designs of his head ornament are drawn from the famed Dunhuang murals, with just a touch of China's traditional lucky designs. Huanhuan is outgoing and enthusiastic. He excels at all the ball games and represents the red Olympic ring.

Yingying is fast and agile and can swiftly cover great stretches of land as he races across the earth. A symbol of the vastness of China's landscape, the antelope carries the blessing of health, the strength of body that comes from harmony with nature. Yingying's running pose captures the essence of a species unique to the Qinghai-Tibet Plateau, one of the first animals put under protection in China. The selection of the Tibetan Antelope reflects Beijing's commitment to green Olympics. His head ornament incorporates several decorative styles from the Qinghai-Tibet and Xinjiang cultures and the ethnic design traditions of western China. Strong in track and field events, Yingying is a quick-witted and agile boy who represents the yellow Olympic ring.

Every spring and summer the children of Beijing fly beautiful kites on the currents of wind that blow through the capital. Among the kite designs, the golden-winged swallow is traditionally one of the most popular. Nini's figure is drawn from this grand tradition of flying designs. Her golden wings symbolize the infinite sky and spread good luck as a blessing wherever she flies. The swallow is also pronounced "yan" in Chinese, and Yanjing is what Beijing was called as an ancient capital city. Among the Fuwas, Nini is as innocent and joyful as a swallow. She is strong in gymnastics and represents the green Olympic ring.

At the heart of their mission, and through all of their work, the Fuwas seek to unite the world in peace and friendship through the Olympic spirit. Dedicated to helping Beijing 2008 spread its theme of "One World, One Dream" to every continent, the Fuwas reflected the deep desire of the Chinese people to reach out to the world in friendship through the Games, and invited every man, woman and child to take part in the great celebration of human solidarity that China hosted in the light of the Olympic flame in 2008.

北京奥运吉祥物——福娃的故事[1]

　　2008 年的北京奥运也让全世界认识了五个拟人化的吉祥物——可爱的福娃！他们名为贝贝、晶晶、欢欢、迎迎、妮妮，谐音为"北京欢迎你"！当然，福娃的设计者，艺术家韩美林也被美誉为"福娃之父"。

　　福娃的设计灵感来自奥运精神的传承与华夏文明的诠释，可谓是"天时地利人和"的最佳表达。如福娃的色彩，取自奥运五环的蓝、黑、红、黄、绿，象征着五大洲的颜色，也是神州乾坤、山川大地、江河湖海的颜色；福娃的形象来自鱼、大熊猫、奥运圣火、藏羚羊及京燕；福娃的造型分别指海洋、森林、圣火、大地和天空，蕴含了"水、木、火、土、金"五行之意。整个设计充满了华夏民族的元素，表达了中国传统文化的精髓，传递了"理解、友谊、团结和公平竞争"的奥林匹克精神。

　　五个福娃突破了历届奥运会吉祥物的数量，展示了中国传统文化与奥林匹克精神的谐和。他们代表着美好的祝愿：繁荣、欢乐、激情、健康、好运，传递了中国人民的好客和首都北京的热情。

---

[1] 关于福娃简介，笔者参阅了新华网及韩美林杭州博物馆相关内容。

Chapter **9**

**Overlooking
the Hometown
—Hangzhou**

家园之美——杭州

Paradise on Earth— Beautiful Hangzhou

After looking at China's map shaped like a rooster, let us enjoy the author's hometown, Hangzhou. It has been likened to "Paradise on Earth", and was the capital of several dynasties, including the Southern Song Dynasty (AD 1127–1279), because of its beautiful and charming landscape. At the beginning of the Yuan Dynasty, the Italian traveller Marco Polo came to Hangzhou and in his travel notes he described Hangzhou as "the most beautiful and luxuriant city of the world". From Hangzhou

© Zhejiang University Press 2016

Yuehong (Helen) Zhang, *Chinese Cultural Kaleidoscope*,

http://dx.doi.org/10.1631/ZUP.B978-7-308-15903-6_ch9

Lingering Snow on the Broken Bridge by F Lu

版画：断桥残雪　作者：陆放

人间天堂——杭州

　　纵观了雄鸡图的大气后，来到笔者工作的浙江大学所在地，素称鱼米之乡的浙江省省会杭州市，自古至今被赞誉为"人间天堂"。话说元朝初年，来到杭州的意大利旅行家马可·波罗在游记中盛赞杭州为"世界上最美丽的华贵之城"。宋朝诗人苏轼写意杭州为"水光潋滟晴方好，山色空蒙雨亦奇。欲把西湖比西子，淡妆浓抹总相宜"，把这个几朝古都的美描写得淋漓尽致，让人流连忘返……

© 浙江大学出版社 2016
张月红，《中国文化万花筒》，
http://dx.doi.org/10.1631/ZUP.B978-7-308-15903-6_ch9

we have the poem "Drinking Wine on the Lake in the Rain after a Sunny Day": Waves glitter in the sunlight; Sunny days are really fine. Mountain sights appear indistinctly; Rainy days are also wonderful. I want to compare the West Lake to Xishi (who is the most beautiful woman in ancient Chinese history); She is always so beautiful. This was written by Su Shi who was a famous poet in Chinese cultural history in the Song Dynasty, whose poem is the real portrait of the West Lake in the beautiful city, Hangzhou.

The author is very fortunate to work in the 119-year-old Zhejiang University, that was one of the earliest universities in China, named as "Qiu Shi Academy" in 1897. This university is located in the beautiful Hangzhou City, capital of Zhejiang Province that has long been known as a fertile and prosperous land with a rich cultural heritage, famous for its silk and West Lake Longjing Tea.

　　创建于 1897 年的浙江大学就位于富庶的浙江省钱塘江边，美丽的杭州西子湖畔。其前身为"求是书院"。

　　论起几朝古都的杭州，除了祭奠这千年沉睡的厚重文化，那西湖的娇美，丝绸的轻柔，还有龙井茶的余香早已是天赐杭州的礼物，地蕴杭州的名片。生活在杭州，游荡了西湖，品尝过龙井，这可是来来往往的杭州人所津津乐道，趣味无穷的享受，那也是人间天堂所给予的厚爱……

Campus of Zhejiang University by B Shen
浙大紫金港校区夜景（沈斌摄）

Longjing Tea Fragrance and Lu Yü's *The Tea Classic*

Because of tea, the powerful Tang Dynasty boasted a strong economy and thriving culture. It was the heyday of ancient Chinese tea culture, which according to historians came into vogue in the Tang Dynasty and flourished in the Song Dynasty. The period saw the introduction of customs and techniques for drinking tea, which would have a far-reaching impact on later generations. In particular, tea became part of everyday life as a major commodity. There appeared many famous varieties, some of which were selected as tribute to the emperor. In particular, it was in this period that taxes began to be levied on tea, and the world's first book on tea *The Tea Classic* was written by Lu Yü (AD 733–804), which was an epoch-making event in the development of Chinese tea culture. In this book, he described that "for tea the mountain-spring water is the best, river water is next best and the well water is slightly

龙井茶香与陆羽的《茶经》

说起绿茶龙井，要追溯到公元 780 年左右，中国茶文化的鼻祖陆羽（733—804），正是他在杭州余杭写出了中国第一部茶学著作——《茶经》。此书的问世，在世界茶文化史上都是浓重的一笔。中国历史上茶业的兴起源于昌盛的大唐，品茶亦成为当朝一种贵族生活的时尚，茶品也随唐朝开拓的丝绸之路远销日本及中亚。生于唐朝的茶圣陆羽，诗人气质浓郁，并精于茶道。 在他论及制茶工具、品茶水质及茶道韵味的 3 卷《茶经》书中娓娓道来，如"用山泉之水润茶最佳，河水尚可，井水略劣"等至今为茶经乐道。而笔者也有幸与民国时杭州有名的三大茶庄之一，方正大（Fang Ching Ta）茶庄有一点渊源——其婆母就出生在方家茶庄

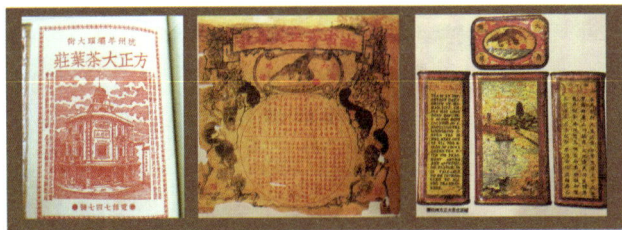

inferior". This book has been regarded as a classic of the Chinese tea ceremony till now.

It so happened that the author has an interesting story about Longjing Tea that is related to the author's family. Her mother-in-law was born into a famous tea merchant's family—Hangzhou's Fang-Ching-Ta that was ranked the No. 3 tea company in the heyday of Hangzhou's tea industry during the Republic of China (AD 1912–1949) described in the book *Hangzhou Tradition Brand: Tea Industry* published by Zhejiang University Press in 2008. From the old pictures (Fang-Ching-Ta's advertisement from the Hangzhou West Lake Expo in 1929 and Fang-Ching-Ta's tea canister), we can know that Fang-Ching-Ta's green tea was exported to the UK and Singapore at that time. As a Hangzhou tea-merchant's daughter, she did not only taste the delicious Longjing Tea and witness its trade blooming, but also deeply believed that Longjing Tea produced in Hangzhou should be the gift that God gives to beautiful Hangzhou, and Hangzhou people should be grateful that this soil is a piece of Heaven on Earth.

（见图：1929年西湖博览会上方正大茶庄广告，取自《杭州老字号——茶业卷》，2008年浙江大学出版社出版）。笔者常饶有兴致地听她说茶，品茶，并知晓她出生之时，正是方正大茶庄兴隆之势，因而见证了方正大的龙井绿茶远销大英帝国、南售新加坡时的红火盛景（见图：印有中英文简介的方正大出口所用的茶罐），更使她深信不疑的是：中国绿茶的头牌——"西湖龙井"，是上帝赐予杭州这片秀丽山水的厚重大礼，杭州人着实懂得感恩这片苍天大地！

Waterside Towns and Scenic Sites Surrounding Hangzhou—Deqing

Guests or travellers who come to Hangzhou are not only deeply impressed by the delicate fragrance of Longjing Tea but also leave with memories of many beautiful ancient waterside towns surrounding the paradise of Hangzhou, with their distinctive features and thousands of years of Chinese civilization. They are Wuzhen town, located to the north-east of Hangzhou, and Xitang town also to the north-east, Nanxun Town to the north of Hangzhou, as well as Shaoxing, Longmen and Deqing near Hangzhou. Actually, it is the beauty of these waterside towns that reflect the beauty of Heaven on Earth—Hangzhou. Take Deqing as an example. Let's enjoy the typical landscape atmosphere and its heritage as a waterside town in southern China.

环绕杭州的水乡之美——德清

来过杭州的乡客，不仅深深迷恋那龙井绿茶淡淡不散的余香，更难以忘怀的是那环绕着人间天堂杭州，沉睡了千古名人，美轮美奂的江南水乡！啊，那种回味真不可言传，只能使乡客们流连忘返……如杭州东北方的乌镇和西塘、正北方的南浔，还有杭州附近的古城绍兴、古镇龙门、小县德清等，正是这些数不清的水乡之美，衬托和映照了人间天堂——杭州的大美！这里不妨信步踏进杭州近邻的德清，来一瞥江南水乡的奇秀与底蕴，饱饱眼福吧。

Located on the northern suburbs of Hangzhou, adjacent to Shanghai, Deqing is neighbored by South Taihu Lake to the north, Tianmu Mountain to the west, and the Southern Wetlands to the east. The exceeding beauty of Deqing flows from the meeting of mountain and water.

Carrying the time-honored culture of China's Grand Canal, and drawing from 5,000 years of Chinese civilization, Deqing's history is both profound and alive.

Xinshi: The ancient town of Xinshi, with more than 1,600 years of history, age-old stone bridges, white walls and black tiles, a reminder of immemorial customs.

Xuguang Pavilion: The elegant Xuguang Pavilion and the various old houses on the scenic Mogan Mountain; a green, quiet and refreshing mountain that enjoys great prestige at home and abroad for its "three wonders"—bamboo, cloud and springs.

Xiazhu Lake: Xiazhu Lake's deep and charming evenings, where the water shares its scenic hue with the vast sky, arousing the imagination.

A Heaven-Sent Gift—Beautiful Deqing.

A Historical Waterside Town Representing 5,000 Years of Chinese Civilization.

古镇新市　　旭光亭　　下渚湖之夜　　雅居莫干

　　德清位于杭州以北，与上海毗邻。北望南太湖，西枕天目山，东孕江南湿地，山水相接，美轮美奂。

　　历史上的德清传承着一段中国大运河源远流淌的文化……吸吮着华夏五千年的文明乳汁，生生不息，厚重清新。

　　恍若千年一叹的水墨画，古镇新市，石桥画榭，粉墙黛瓦，古风犹存。

　　雍贵万千的旭光亭和风光奇异的山墅民居在以竹、云、泉"三美"和绿、凉、静"三绝"而蜚声海内外的莫干山中若隐若现。

　　镶嵌在湿地一隅的下渚湖，更是天水一色，深邃迷人，令你遐想万千。这真是：

　　天赐德清，奇山美水秀乡。

　　地蕴古镇，千史名流沉睡。

Concluding Remarks
后　记

An academic journal editor's cultural expression

When it comes to this book, it is necessary to say that it was my career as an academic journal editor that let me start to explore our 5,000 years of culture and be proud of its heritage and beauty. It is important to have a strong drive to express and spread our profound Chinese culture though I am ashamed that my own understanding of Chinese culture is very limited.

Back in 2003, I was a managing editor of *Journal of Zhejiang University-SCIENCE* that had already been funded for three years as a new journal and was carrying out the international peer reviewing system in order to make it become an international publication. As reported by ALPSP (Association of Learned & Professional Society Publishers), "It was one of the first Chinese-based journals to introduce truly international peer reviewing systems in 2003 in order to ensure its high quality. And up until 2013, from its website 'Int'l reviewer' (http://

© Zhejiang University Press 2016

Yuehong (Helen) Zhang, *Chinese Cultural Kaleidoscope*,

http://dx.doi.org/10.1631/ZUP.B978-7-308-15903-6_conclusion

一个学术期刊编辑的文化表达

有人说："身边的，就是世界的。"我说："历史的文化，就是人类的文化，无论发生在何时、何地，归属全世界，也即你、我、他……"

这本书的出版与笔者的职业有关。多年来，笔者一直担任《浙江大学学报》三份英文学术期刊（JZUS-A 辑：《应用物理与工程》；JZUS-B 辑：《生物医学与生物工程》；JZUS-C 辑：计算机与电子，现更名为 FITEE《信息与电子工程前沿》）的总编辑。其间，笔者与编辑同仁，努力着把这几本中国办的英文学术期刊推向世界。创刊的第一步是邀请全球的学术同行为本刊投稿论文审稿，即全方位的国际同行评审体系始于 2003 年。几年下来，为期刊学术把脉的 26000 多位学者来自 69 个国家和地区（见本刊在线的国际审稿专家库名单录：http://www.zju.edu.cn/jzus/reviewer.php）。正是这些默默做出学术贡献的国际学者，让本刊的作者与读者等在学术交流中认可了这三份学术刊物。

©浙江大学出版社 2016
张月红，《中国文化万花筒》，
http://dx.doi.org/10.1631/ZUP.B978-7-308-15903-6_conclusion

www.zju.edu.cn/jzus/reviewer.php),more than 26,000 referees from 69 countries and regions have provided a review service for *JZUS*."

During that time, all the editors very much appreciated these scientists, researchers and experts as peer reviewers. We wanted to express our compliments and sincere thanks to these scholars or reviewers. As Confucius said "Give me a peach, I will send you a good wine" in his *The Book of Songs*. Thus, I reminded myself that our rich culture might be interesting to these scholars and reviewers. So, from 2003 to 2015, I have personally compiled a series of cultural booklets on different subjects. They are as follows:

- The civilization of China—its fascinating culture;
- The land of China—its geography and people;
- Chinese philosophy—six ancient Chinese thinkers of the Pre-Qin Period;
- Chinese festivals culture;
- Chinese folk culture—good fortune, prosperity, longevity, happiness;

　　起初，笔者问自己，深受中国几千年感恩文化的熏陶，何以致谢这些为本刊迈向世界而默默做出学术贡献的幕后审稿功臣？这让笔者想到了悠悠几千年厚重的中国文化犹如万花筒一样多姿多彩，如若把不同主题的华夏文明做成别有价值的文化小名片，并将这礼物在圣诞前夜悄悄放在接收者的信箱里，当他或她一打开，莫不是一种节日的惊喜？！之余细细品来，那更是一种沁人心扉的文化享受！是的，许许多多的国外学者来信表达了这种喜悦与感谢，当然更多的是对中国文化的惊叹与欣赏（见英文摘录）。其中一位法国学者说："我儿子看到中国书法文化册，直说'我想去中国看看字，该有多么的美！'"

　　这些年，笔者工作之余，喜欢醉于中国文化小名片的编撰之中。坦率地说，一旦触摸到厚重灿烂的华夏文明的积淀，常常喟叹与汗颜作为中华子民对文化根基了解的浅与薄。虽是胆大地先后编撰了十几个主题文化册，如华夏文明、神州大地、中国古典文学选集、中国古典建筑选集、文房四宝、中国书法、民俗文化——十二生肖与福禄寿喜、中国书画四君子——梅兰竹菊、中国"年"（节日）文化、中国哲学——先秦时代的六大思想家、北京奥运文化等，当然也不忘一叙生活之地的"天堂杭州与江南水

- Chinese folk culture—the Chinese zodiac;
- Chinese classical literature—selections;
- Chinese buildings and structures—selections;
- Chinese calligraphy;
- Four treasures of study in China—writing brush, inkstick, paper and inkstone;
- The "four gentlemen" in Chinese painting culture—plum, orchid, bamboo, and chrysanthemum;
- The Beijing Olympic Games in 2008;

...

Also, we wanted not only to let these booklets introduce our rich Chinese culture, but also to express our thanks by providing with the booklets a small gift in the form of recently issued Chinese stamps that portray aspects of Chinese culture. This gesture was described on the ALPSP site (Association of Learned & Professional Society Publishers) at http://blog.alpsp.org, entitled "Innovation versus very good journals in 2014" as follows:

"Rather than aiming for anonymous 'international' status, it is conscious of its roots, and celebrates the

乡",着实说来是力不从心！但为了践行以中国文化来致谢国际审稿学者这个初衷，虽然生涩，但却炽热地出手了这十几本文化小册。今天将它们编撰成书，实不敢忘记自己是学习者。

回首十几年来用文化小册表达感恩的小举，不仅给海内外学者们送去了一份暖暖的华夏子民的人文情怀，也得到国际学术出版业的一个首肯，如2014年8月全球学术与专业出版者协会（ALPSP）在其官方月报与博客中这样评说"特别要提这份中国期刊（*JZUS*）在默默耕耘'国际化'进程中，心系文化之根，用源远流长的五千年中国文化来致敬国际审稿人，向世界传播一种国家文化……"

此刻，就想把这些年"浅浅"的"文化表达"编撰成这本小书——《中国文化万花筒》，作为小礼物，献给全世界喜欢中国文化的大人和孩子们，闲来一阅解奇，一睹为快。书名中的"万花筒（Kaleidoscope）"一词，寓意上下五千年的华夏文明，其每一个触角都是一个绚丽的光点，千千万万个光点交相辉映，折射出中华民族文化的灿烂、历史的沧桑、民俗的美妙……当我们面对这些色彩斑斓，变化万千的中国元素，烙在心底就是感动、感谢和感恩！

cultural heritage of China. Chinese cultural tokens are used to reward its reviewers, wherever in the world they are..."

Also over these years we received expressions of thanks from these scholars:

Here are some examples:

A professor from the USA, who said, "This is a gracious and charming gesture in a professional world that is often too brusque and impersonal."

One from the UK: "I received today the very beautiful 'Four Treasures of Study' set of stamps you sent to my address. I thought it was kind and remarkable of you to recognize my review in this fashion. Thank you very, very much!"

One from Italy: "I would like to thank you for the wonderful booklet on Chinese Philosophy that you sent me. It is so interesting and so beautiful! I appreciated very much the stamps with the famous Chinese philosophers and the information in the text."

One from Australia: "I have just received the booklet you sent me before Christmas. Thank you as I was

是也，感恩也是我们文化的根系，正如《诗经》中言之："投我以木桃，报之以琼瑶。"正是中华感恩文化的一句至理名言。

文化是一个人的根，无论你走得多远，它一直牵着你……

away. They are great to have and I admire the Chinese philosophers' teachings."

This is the background to this book.

Culture is at the heart of a person who should be proud of his / her rich cultural heritage.

中華上下五千年

中國文化萬花筒

A five-millennium's history

Chinese Cultural Kaleidoscope